PRAISE FOR

TO STOP A TYRANT

"*To Stop a Tyrant* is not a politicized screed to enable the partisan fractures of the moment. It is a powerful invitation to be a better informed and engaged citizen. A must-read for how political tyranny can be preempted before it arrives in the halls of power."

—THE HONORABLE DAVID A. HARDY, PhD.,
judge, Washoe County, NV

"Ira Chaleff offers us an incisive study for our times, encouraging contemplation of our ethical values as followers and the choice to stand on the sidelines or stand up and courageously nudge our leaders to act in accordance with those values."

—JAY EAGEN, chief administrative officer,
United States House of Representatives (retired)

"What insightful analysis and practical guidance for how followers in every circle can take a stand for democracy! A brilliant piece of scholarship arriving at exactly the right moment."

—DR. MAX KLAU, senior advisor,
New Politics Leadership Academy

"So relevant! *To Stop a Tyrant* is the wakeup call for the perilous times we are living in. Chaleff challenges us to tap into our courageous follower superpowers and be this generation's effective agents of political change."

— **WENDY EDMONDS**, Ph.D., author of
Intoxicating Followership in the Jonestown Massacre

"*To Stop a Tyrant* masterfully navigates the complex political landscape with a refreshingly non-partisan approach. The deeply prescient observations in this book could not be more timely."

—**KRISH RAVAL**, OBE, Director of
Faith in Leadership, United Kingdom

"George Santayana admonished, 'Those who forget the past are condemned to repeat it.' Remembering is the first requirement: Courageous actions must follow. Ira Chaleff provides a toolbox to intervene before tyranny once more turns civilizations to rubble. I can't help but contemplate what the 20th century could have been had this book been available then."

—**ANNE R. Z. SCHULMAN**, Holocaust educator and author

TO STOP A TYRANT

Published by Wonderwell Press
Austin, Texas
www.gbgpress.com

This work is being published under the Wonderwell Press imprint by an exclusive arrangement with Wonderwell. Wonderwell, Wonderwell Press, and the Wonderwell logos are wholly-owned trademarks of Wonderwell.

Distributed by Greenleaf Book Group

For ordering information or special discounts for bulk purchases, please contact Greenleaf Book Group at PO Box 91869, Austin, TX 78709, 512.891.6100.

Design and composition by Greenleaf Book Group and Adrian Morgan
Cover design by Greenleaf Book Group
Cover Art: Adobe Stock
Interior Art: Photo of people sitting in a circle.
Copyright © David Hancock / Alamy Stock Photo
Photo of August Landmesser.
Copyright © Niday Picture Library / Alamy Stock Photo
Photo of Baltic Chain. Copyright © by Laimonis Stīpnieks
Publisher's Cataloging-in-Publication data is available.

Print ISBN: 978-1-63756-056-3

eBook ISBN: 978-1-63756-057-0

To offset the number of trees consumed in the printing of our books, Greenleaf donates a portion of the proceeds from each printing to the Arbor Day Foundation. Greenleaf Book Group has replaced over 50,000 trees since 2007.

Printed in the United States of America on acid-free paper

24 25 26 27 28 29 30 31   10 9 8 7 6 5 4 3 2 1

First Edition

TO STOP A TYRANT

THE POWER OF POLITICAL FOLLOWERS
TO MAKE OR *BRAKE* A TOXIC LEADER

IRA CHALEFF

WONDERWELL
PRESS

To my maternal grandmother, Sarah Ellenberg Temkin,
who lost her entire family in the Holocaust
during the Second World War,
a heinous crime perpetrated by tyrannical leaders
and by the followers who enabled them to rise to power.

CONTENTS

PREFACE

There is anxiety in the land. This is true in many countries that have considered themselves liberal democracies, however imperfect.

A survey of the global political landscape shows a regression to authoritarian rule. Whether you fear this encroachment is coming from "the left" or "the right," you are correct to be concerned, even disturbed. Unchecked, these trends can alter public life as we know it and, eventually, our private lives as well.

You may be equally disturbed by the number of your fellow citizens accepting or supporting these toxic authoritarian trends. But that is the very essence of toxicity: Rather than limiting damage to a specific organ, it poisons the entire system. In the political body, this includes a large percentage of the leader's supporters.

Ultimately, no leader—good, bad, weak, or strong—achieves anything without the cooperation of the people they inspire, persuade, seduce, or coerce into following them. This book will help you understand and potentially alter this enabling behavior.

While it appears that leaders create their followers, it is equally true that followers create their leaders. A few of us can directly reach and influence a political leader of a major city, state, province, or nation. All of us can exert influence through various channels and strategies, particularly in a democracy, if we recognize how it is in our best interest to do so.

Many of us would rather live our lives focusing on our own challenges and aspirations than devote energy to influencing or checking political leaders. They're paid good money to care for public business, and we expect them to do so. But reality intervenes. We find they are going in directions that may adversely affect our lives, so we become motivated to do something about it. In fact, this is good. Otherwise, our political muscles atrophy, and with them, so do our democratic rights.

Over a quarter century ago, I began to study, write, and teach about the follower role in group life—a much more influential role than is commonly believed. My books have found their way into bastions of hierarchy in many fields and countries. This journey began decades earlier, as a child learning of the Holocaust. Why did people follow monstrous leaders? That child is still asking that question but has learned some of the answers. This book is designed to share those insights and stimulate further thinking.

Drawing on my decades of interaction with political leaders, the staff who support them, the constituents they serve, and new research within the active, global follower-ship community, I will offer thoughts on timely resistance when leaders weaken appropriate checks on their power.

The term *followership* may be new to you. It will become clearer as you see its application throughout the book. For the moment, envision this: Leading requires someone to follow. On the dance floor, one partner leads, and the other follows. The beauty of the dance requires both partners to play their roles well. If we value good leadership, then it makes sense to value good followership. This is equally true off the dance floor in any group activity, including the political.

A useful difference between this book and others exam-ining the erosion of democracy is its identification of steps any political follower can take to thwart that erosion. Steps *you* can take.

I came of age in the 1960s, when many in my generation followed charismatic leaders claiming to have the answers to life that remedy the dysfunctions so prevalent in human society. We perceived the injustices embedded in societal systems and the existential threat posed by technology such as nuclear arsenals. We calculated, however naively, that usual strategies for transforming the system would not work in time to avoid disaster. This primed us to accept seductive claims by political charismatics (or religious and new age saviors) that answers lay outside politics as usual. Perhaps these conditions sound familiar today.

This experience allowed me to understand the thrall of charismatic figures viscerally. It has served me well in my life's work: exploring the healthy and unhealthy relationships between followers and leaders, between those who place their faith in a larger-than-life figure—the supposed "savior" who is then transformed by power from a shepherd to a wolf.

We may be tempted to judge those who fall under the sway of a charismatic figure and their underlying authoritarianism. Having been there, I know the futility of making judgments. Rather, I try performing as a lifeguard, warning swimmers of the dangerous undertow and how to overcome its pull.

We can rationalize away questionable acts of a charismatic leader in whom we place great faith. Eventually, we reach a tipping point when the strain of explaining away the troubling behavior is too great, and we must reevaluate what we are experiencing. In the political arena, it is important to do this while there is still the freedom to disagree, dissent, and diverge.

When I gained distance from the authoritarian ethos, I used the experience to understand the darker movements in history: those in which followers succumbed to or enabled power-hungry leaders to control the coercive levers of government. Based on my three decades of experience in Washington, DC, and global democracy building, I am offering observations on how the interactions between political followers and leaders can work well and how they go awry. I have attempted to ground my general observations in mini vignettes of political and social reality. This presents several challenges.

In the first instance, some of the vignettes will be from periods when a tyrant has already consolidated power, as these are better documented than periods before it is clear a tyrant is emerging. Yet, it is crucial to be alert to the early warning signs of a metamorphosis from political leader to political tyrant.

Second, these are snapshots. Circumstances in contemporary examples will have evolved by the time you read this book. When using these examples, actions taken may have proven to have been in vain. There are no guarantees of success when acting, only of preserving one's integrity.

Third, I use these vignettes as one might use a palate cleanser between the courses of a meal to avoid one point running into another. They are not in-depth case histories. This may irk a reader who has a more sophisticated understanding of an example used than I do or may have a different interpretation. At times, to sidestep these challenges, I have chosen to use a hypothetical or composite vignette and will flag these as such.

I wish I could label these examples as belonging only to history. But similar dark forces continue to percolate through contemporary events. This book explores how to keep those forces from defining our future.

While writing this book, friends would ask what it was about. When I told them it was a book about stopping a political tyrant, they would inevitably say, "Boy, is that timely!" My response was, yes, it is timely. But it has always been timely throughout human history. I am writing to explore how we, as political followers, might influence or change this recurring destructive phenomenon.

Some of my friends may question why I am not using examples from the ongoing race for the next US president: examples of the political right's fears of Joe Biden weaponizing the Administrative State and the political left's fears of Donald Trump dismantling democratic safeguards. My answer to this is clear: I am writing about the power of *followers* to elevate a toxic leader or to put on the "brakes" and interrupt their rise to power—not in tomorrow's election, but in *any* age.

When I was director of the nonpartisan Congressional Management Foundation, it was not my job to tell the electorate whom to send to Congress but rather to help those they elected effectively understand their constituents' needs and serve them well. I am not making it my job to tell anyone whom to support but to better equip them to use their power to choose political leaders thoughtfully, get the best from them, and avoid enabling any latent or visible toxicity.

I leave it to the reader as a citizen, regardless of partisan preference, to take what they find useful in this book and apply it to the contemporary political figures they support, worry about, or oppose. If the reader does that, I will have done my work while honoring theirs. It is the reader and their actions that will make this book applicable to the current political moment. This means *you*. Meanwhile, the book will continue to be relevant to future generations of courageous followers who apply its principles to the political leaders of *their* time and place.

IRA CHALEFF | June 2024

INTRODUCTION

The world is awash in political tyrants and would-be tyrants—so is human history. We are no closer to eliminating this scourge of the political organization of societies.

The remedies for removing a tyrant who has consolidated power are dire, and the consequences of failure are unspeakable. What can be done—what must be done—is to detect and dismantle the ascension of the tyrant while events can be influenced, short of civil war or revolution. That is the project of these pages.

These same dynamics can play out at any level of government. For some readers, those at a local level will have a greater impact on their lives or at least appear realistically to be more within their power to influence. This is an equally valid lens through which to read the material in this book. Nevertheless, the worst tyrants are those who grab the power of a nation-state and use it to impose their will on everyone within its jurisdiction.

Merriam-Webster defines a *tyrant* as follows:

(1a): an absolute ruler unrestrained by law or constitution

(b): a usurper of sovereignty

(2a): a ruler who exercises absolute power oppressively or brutally

(b): one resembling an oppressive ruler in the harsh use of authority or power

The scope of this book will embrace the definitions offered in 1a, b, and 2a. There may well be lessons that pertain to the wider use of the word as per 2b that reaches beyond the political sphere. But our focus will be squarely on the power of followers of the political ruler to check or to magnify their abuses of office.

FOLLOWERS

There is an underlying structure to all human political organization, whether the system is one of the many varieties of democracy or autocracy. This structure is what we generally refer to as *leaders and followers*.

The unique lens of this book is its focus not on the tyrant but on their followers. However destructive tyrants are, they would be impotent without followers, willing or coerced to execute their designs. While this is true, it is an insufficient analysis. Followers have different degrees of motivation, power, and responsibilities depending on their proximity to the leader. This differential has been largely overlooked in the fields of followership and political leadership. We will examine the distinctive circles of followers in different proximity to the leader, who, if unchecked, would become a tyrant.

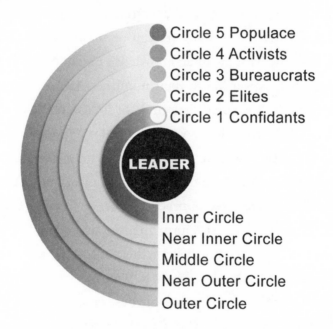

Circle 5 Populace
Circle 4 Activists
Circle 3 Bureaucrats
Circle 2 Elites
Circle 1 Confidants

LEADER

Inner Circle
Near Inner Circle
Middle Circle
Near Outer Circle
Outer Circle

THE FIVE CIRCLES OF FOLLOWERS

I will refer to an authoritarian political figure as a *prototyrant*. They may or may not develop into full tyrannical power, but they have the shape-shifting potential to do so. For this to occur, five different types of followers must provide more tacit acceptance of this transformation than resistance to it. Each type of follower holds a different source of power that can be used to support, influence, retard, or magnify the transition to tyrant.

The five circles occupy increasingly closer proximity to the political leader. Individuals may, at times, find themselves in different circles as their relationship with the leader changes through a variety of mechanisms we will explore. We are all in at least one of these circles.

The fifth circle of followers can be viewed as the outer ring, with the least personal knowledge of and access to the leader. Their power lies in their numbers. At the other end of the scale is the small first circle of followers. This is the "inner circle," which is privy to the private conversations and behavior of the leader and who, theoretically, has the most opportunity to influence them. For reasons we shall see, theory isn't always realized in practice.

All classifications are approximations and simplifications of more complex realities. Nevertheless, they help us name and better understand a variety of phenomena. I have chosen the following descriptions for these classifications.

The Outer Circle—The Populace: The people living in the governed area, the supposed beneficiaries of good government. We can loosely use the more common term *citizenry*, though noncitizens who live under the government's jurisdiction are included in this circle.

The Near Outer Circle—Activists: The highly committed individuals and groups who activate and organize segments of the citizenry in support of or against political leaders and their policies.

The Operational Circle—Government Bureaucrats: The legions of professionals and administrators who operate the levers of government under the direction of political leaders. They translate policies into programs that affect wide areas of our lives.

The Near Inner Circle—Elites and Influencers: Business leaders, media giants, financial market movers, legislative powerhouses, judicial arbiters, cultural tastemakers, and others who can command the attention of the other circles of followers and that of the leader.

The Inner Circle—Confidants: Family, old friends, mega-financiers, senior staff, and favorite loyalists who have the ear of the leader.

Those in the inner circle have a more immediate perception of the leader's thinking, behavior, passions, and blind spots. The near inner circle has a slightly more removed perspective and different types of data and insight. Bureaucrats are the unseen hand that methodically implements policies . . . or not. Those in the outer circles have different perspectives still.

Where we are in relation to the leader and what data we can see gives us different perspectives, tools, and responsibilities for responding to changes in the leader's behavior. We will examine these circles to understand their motivations, power, potential to influence events, fears, vulnerabilities, and incentives for collusion that they often come to regret.

At times we may move closer or further away from

the leader by reason of our commitment, assignments we accept, the leader promoting or demoting us, the need for our expertise, and the shifting landscape of other leaders or events. Therefore, even though one of the spheres is most germane to you at this moment, it is useful to have knowledge of the dynamics of followership in each of the spheres.

THE THREE BEHAVIORS OF FOLLOWERS

In his doctoral dissertation,[1] Dr. Alain de Sales, a colleague of mine in Australia who has built on my work, identifies three essential types of follower behavior in the face of toxic leadership:

- *Conformist followers* go about their business, falling in line with whatever dictates emanate from the toxic leader.

- *Colluder followers* actively enable the toxic leader, even amplifying their toxicity.

- *Courageous followers* seek ways to counteract the toxicity, including removing the destructive leader if necessary.

We will examine the characteristics of toxic political leadership shortly. For the moment, it is important to understand that these three types of follower behavior can and do occur in each circle of followership. To stop a political tyrant will require enough courageous followership to outmaneuver the conformity and collusion on which an emerging tyrant depends.

WHY FOLLOWERS?

Why focus on the follower rather than on the emerging tyrannical leader? National, state or provincial political leaders command the overwhelming might of surveillance, taxation, policing, and military power. Surely, we must focus on their values, competence, emotional balance, and, most especially, sanity to weed out the authoritarian personality who may metamorphize into a tyrant.

While it is not necessarily a fool's errand to identify the characteristics of an emerging tyrant, it is an extremely fraught exercise. Any list of the characteristics of a tyrant can be interpreted through the eyes of the emerging tyrant's followers or the opposition. They will reach different assessments of whether their leader (to date, most often a man) displays tyrannical characteristics or the qualities of a savior.

In hindsight, we think that the rising tyrant was always recognizable. In practice, for those living through contemporary events, it may not have been as clear to all the ancillary actors. Or, the perceived benefits the individual brought to office in the specific context of the times might have been cause to overlook or be willfully blind to worrisome flaws.

Yes, there are those power seekers brazen enough to foreshadow their destructive political agendas in virulent treatises—*Mein Kampf* being the iconic example. Yes, these should be taken more seriously than history shows they have been. However, emerging tyrants do not necessarily preview the extent of their ruthlessness until they have amassed sufficient power to do so openly. Because autocrats find fertile ground in uncertain and difficult times (when people look for a savior), many readily mistake the strong man for that savior. They see what they wish to see and discount the warning flares.

Instead of offering a book presuming to turn us into amateur psychologists able to predict the trajectory of political figures with oversized egos, I suggest we look at ourselves, the potential followers, for the information we need to better discern and interrupt unwanted outcomes. This shifts the locus of our attention onto the aspect of the follower–leader relationship over which we have direct control. When followers resolutely change their behavior in relationship to the leader—*if this is done before the leader acquires unassailable power*—it is the leader who then needs to make adjustments if they are to keep their followers. I invite you to look at the follower role from the vantage point of each of the circles into which events and our actions may thrust us.

TYRANTS NOT TYRANNY

This book is about the relationship of followers to tyrants, not to tyranny. These are distinct. The political tyrant is an individual who co-opts the resources and power of the State, using it to control its citizens and turn them into agents of their venomous reign. Tyranny is not embodied in an individual but rather takes the form of oppression embedded in a system: the tyranny of racism, sexism, poverty, and the like. Analyses of the complex forces comprising these oppressive dynamics are beyond the scope of this book. However, they may be affected by the success or failure of efforts to limit the power of the emerging tyrant.

PEOPLE NOT POLICY

This book is about people, not policy. More specifically, it is about how people are susceptible to would-be tyrants and what we can do about that. It is not a discussion of policy initiatives that reduce the fertile field for autocrats to take root or that limit how they can consolidate their power. Those topics and initiatives are hugely important but beyond the scope of this project. They also tend to quickly become laundry lists with insufficient attention to the political realities of implementation. Suggestions for these can be found elsewhere.[2] Here, we will focus on what we, as individual actors, can do, whether from our modest platform or a more elevated leverage point in our social system.

This book invites us to create a standard of following in which we are effective guardians of our political freedoms. This begins with alertness to our tendency to wish a heroic leader into existence who will resolve all that we see wrong in the world. Of course, we wish that. It is a beautiful longing. Yet, that idealistic wish allows the strongman to capture our better natures and turn them into tools for his ambitions of ultimate power.

PROTOTYRANT, NOT ENTRENCHED TYRANT

I will be referring to the autocratic leader as a *prototyrant*. *Proto* refers to the early emergence of a characteristic, signs that something is arising, is coming into being. A similar word is *prototype*. The dictionary defines *prototype* as "an individual that exhibits the essential features of a later type."

Prototyrants have not amassed the power to issue tyrannical orders and effectively enforce their execution. But the historical or current signs of their inclination to do so are becoming evident. The political prototyrant's actions and policies move determinedly in the direction of weakening the power of any societal or governance institution not under their direct control. This is a warning sign of the intention to accumulate more power than needed to serve people well—too much to be trusted in the hands of an ambitious power wielder.

It can be argued that the greater problem by far is the entrenched tyrant, not what I am referring to as the *prototyrant*. It is they whose policies and actions oppress, enslave, or murder large numbers of people. While this is true, the remedies to displace the entrenched tyrant are of a different magnitude that bleeds into extralegal, revolutionary, and clandestine international intrigue. These are the fare for desperate underground cabals, not for readers of thoughtful books seeking prophylactic measures against tyrannical trajectories.

This book will raise awareness of each circle of political followership that we may occupy in relation to rising political leaders with authoritarian tendencies. It will focus on the pressures found in each circle and the choices available for interrupting the metamorphosis and ascension of a tyrant. In other words, what can be done within the norms of available, legitimate processes in the political moment that allow the publication of a book such as the one now in your hands?

INTERRUPTING THE
PROTOTYRANT'S PROGRESSION

When fires are small, we can smother them with a blanket or a bucket of sand. When they become conflagrations, all we can do is escape with our lives, retreat, and attempt to create fire breaks. So it is with the escalation of a leader with authoritarian tendencies to one who becomes a full-blown tyrant. By focusing on our responses as followers, we may be able to contain the flame at the heart of this leader within the bounds of a well-regulated furnace that serves our needs. Or, we may learn the fire refuses containment and must be extinguished by withdrawing the fuel of followership while it is within our power to do so.

Window for Interrupting the Progression from Autocrat to Tyrant

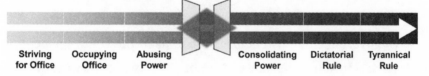

| Striving for Office | Occupying Office | Abusing Power | | Consolidating Power | Dictatorial Rule | Tyrannical Rule |

The time to act is in the window after abuse of power shows up and before the autocrat has time to consolidate power and eliminate all challenges to his rule.

Depending on the historical context, that window may take months or more to close, but in the hands of a prototyrant, it will close. We will examine the signs that require determined action while it can still be effective.

That action is not necessarily to remove a prototyrant from their candidacy or office. This may only create chaos if other less talented and more ferocious political figures are waiting in the wings. At times, it may be possible—and preferable—for followers at every level of society to attempt to contain the excesses of an autocratic personality while using the talents that propelled them to regional or national leadership. In other words, to put a *brake* on the prototyrannical progression, bringing it to a stop while leaving the vehicle itself still capable of performing its legitimate functions.

THE CASE OF THE WOULD-BE DICTATOR

It is sometimes easier to see the fundamentals of political dynamics as they play out in a culture other than our own. While this book frequently references the historic political culture in the United States, where it is being written, it also draws on parallels in other political cultures. Partly, this is in service to those confronting these dynamics in their systems of governance. It also helps those of us in the US to see better fracture lines in our system of guarding against the rise of tyrannical rule and to consider their potential antidotes.

In 2001, given my experience with the US Congress, I was asked to go to Nigeria to facilitate a strategic planning session for the leadership of the newly formed Senate. Nigeria is the largest country in Africa, with over two hundred million people. It had a recurring history of democratic rule, followed by periods of military dictatorship. The hope this time was that a democratic culture would take root and continue to elect successive administrations that shared power with the legislature, courts, and state governments.

When I arrived, I was whisked into a luncheon with

several Senate party leaders. Despite jet lag, I wanted to humanize our relationship rather than let it remain a formal one between facilitator and retreat participants. One of the senators, who seemed to be comfortable with less formality, was Saidu Muhammed Dansadau. He had a reputation for being independent and outspoken about government failures, including those of his party. We quickly bonded.

As in all large political entities, Nigeria was riven by competing political factions. Its boundaries had been arbitrarily drawn under colonial rule and contained three significant tribal groups and many smaller ones. In addition, the Northern part of the created nation was largely Muslim and poorer than the Christian South. In 1968, these tensions erupted into what became known as the Biafran Civil War. Due to direct casualties and blockades of food supplies, it is estimated that as many as two million people died of starvation. The images of skeletal mothers and children seared themselves into public consciousness around the world.

When I conducted a ranked values exercise with the new Senate leadership, the two values that towered above all others for them were "national unity" and "fear of God." Given the memory and deep trauma of their sectarian civil war, do you see the importance of the first and the tension with the second, which required wise and fair governance?

The new constitution—modeled on that of the US—and the norms that grew around it spoke to these governing imperatives. Rather than create a two-party system, like in the US, Nigeria has three primary national parties, mainly formed around tribal identity. Each were expected to run candidates in every state to reduce polarization between sections of the country in which the different tribal groups and religious faiths were dominant and regional economic interests prevailed. People who were thoughtful about governing were making serious attempts to create a viable democracy and avoid the concentration of power that plagues so many postcolonial African countries.

In addition to my facilitating the strategic planning retreat, my host arranged for me to conduct a seminar based on my book *The Courageous Follower* for senior legislative staff. *The Courageous Follower* offers a model in which the willingness to support a leader is balanced with the readiness to challenge their problematic blind spots or misuses of power. My host distributed copies of the book to the staff and several of the senators. Both the seminar and the facilitated retreat produced significant engagement. Months later, back in the US, I received expressions of appreciation, including a grateful letter from Senator Dansadau, on the benefits of the retreat.

A couple of years later, at the beginning of the second term of President Olusegun Obasanjo, I was asked to return to Nigeria as part of a larger team to engage the entire Senate in a three-day symposium on further strengthening the legislative branch of government. At breakfast on the second day, a senator who chaired the communications committee approached me. Seeing my name tag, he introduced himself. The Senator told me that President Obasanjo had presented him with an inscribed copy of *The Courageous Follower* and had given another copy to the head of the government personnel office. With great pride, he told me that he kept the book by his bedside. Then, quite innocently, he added that he had made many copies for his friends! Leaving aside the question of intellectual property rights, there are few things more encouraging for an author to hear than the ideas in his books were gaining such high-level circulation.

Later, the story came full circle. The office of the president of Nigeria, similar to that of the president of the US, is not ceremonial: It is a true power center. The president is both head of government and head of state, as well as commander in chief of the military. With this much power concentrated in one individual, the constitution imposed a four-year, two-term limit. To the disappointment of many who had largely appreciated President Obasanjo's administrations, he initiated a campaign to revise this constitutional constraint and be allowed to run for a third successive term.

Senator Dansadau, a member of the National Assembly Joint Committee of the Review of the Constitution, was a strong opponent of allowing the president to run for a third term. He announced he would boycott a public hearing on the review of the 1999 constitution, which would allow this change. Other political figures within Nigeria, including Obasanjo's cabinet members, as well as political leaders in the global community, also opposed weakening this constitutional constraint on power. Obasanjo withdrew from his efforts to consolidate power.

The Nigerian press captured this well in the article "Obasanjo's Aides Worked Against 3rd Term":

In a move likely to jolt political observers and allies of former President Olusegun Obasanjo, Senator Saidu Muhammad Dansadau has said that some of Obasanjo's former ministers and special advisers had aligned with members of the last National Assembly to truncate the tenure elongation bid allegedly nursed by the former president.

Before now, Nigerians had hailed members of the anti-third term movement, notably members of the National Assembly and other opposition elements within and outside the ruling PDP, but no one knew of the efforts of the former President's cabinet in the whole saga, which culminated in the defeat of the agenda on May 16, 2006, at the floor of the Senate.[3]

THE POWER FIREBREAK

In this example from Nigeria, political followers from several circles around the president interrupted the extraconstitutional attempt to consolidate power. This is exactly the way a *power firebreak* should operate. While there is political space to do so, extinguish what threatens to become a conflagration that would consume the appropriate distribution of power. When actors from different circles of followers come together to interrupt that trajectory, the system can restore the balance needed for the responsible use of power.

The importance of this timely act should not be underestimated. As of this writing, Nigeria has now had four successive legal presidential transitions of power. In a continent struggling with autocrats who have managed to consolidate dictatorial power and often rule as tyrants for life, this is an exception to celebrate and emulate. This does not mean Nigeria is an exemplary model of governance— far from it. This means that the extrajudicial terror so often found under strongman rule is minimized, and space exists to continue improving the mechanisms of governance. Here on Earth, this is no small accomplishment.

In the following chapters, we will explore the forces that need to be understood and managed for a healthy resistance to the excess consolidation of power in political systems, including our own. In the final chapter, using the iconic examples of the *Pentagon Papers* and the Watergate burglary and cover-up during the Nixon administration, we will look at how all the circles of followers coming together can interrupt the trajectory of a leader who demonstrates the signs of becoming a tyrannical ruler, unconstrained by law or custom.

Leading and following always occur within a specific context—a dance floor, an organization, a democracy. We will begin the first chapter by examining important and unique qualities of followership in the political arena.

CHAPTER 1

FOLLOWERS IN A

POLITICAL CONTEXT

.

"The most important thing in a democracy is followers.
That's what democracy is."
—JOANNE CIULLA, leadership ethics philosopher

THE STRUCTURE OF POLITICAL
LEADING AND FOLLOWING

Political matters affect far more aspects of our lives than we
think. Given this reality, understanding the fundamentals of
political dynamics is of personal importance.

There is an underlying structure to all political organization, whether the system is one of the many variations of
democracy or autocracy. This structure is what we generally
refer to as *leaders and followers*. It is fundamentally wired
into human social existence and is more complex than the

relationship captured by those general categories. By recognizing the structure of this system, understanding its value, and identifying its vulnerabilities and leverage points, we may be able to alter our approach to leadership and followership at all levels of political organization.

As in most things in life, the relationship between political leading and following is a double-edged sword: It can produce the framework in which communal life flourishes, or it can create conditions of scarcity, hardship, and oppression. When it flourishes, leading and following roles are more fluid, transferring between different individuals with the skills to provide leadership in specific, changing contexts. When it becomes oppressive, the leader's role entrenches itself and relies increasingly on coercion and fear.

While different for each culture and period, the general willingness to follow, whether freely or under compulsion, is deeply ingrained. This trait has powered the extraordinary accomplishments that large groups of humans have been able to make. It has also contributed to the devastating injustices and crimes committed by humans against each other in all parts of the world and all periods of history. There is a legitimate question whether these destructive tendencies can be changed, whether they can evolve. For the sake of our common future, we must assume this is possible while recognizing the deep forces that will resist change.

There is a need for a shared sense of national purpose for the larger group to succeed in relation to its own needs and to its competitors or adversaries. Followers must have a degree of belief in their leaders, a degree of commitment to their vision, and a willingness to support its implementation, even if it is not everything they might wish it to be. At the same time, the dark side of followership may be operative—the tendency to rationalize away destructive leadership behavior, which should be confronted for what it is, as should the tendency to transfer one's moral accountability onto the leader and the regime. We will explore how humanity can maintain the evolutionary advantage of large-scale, coordinated followership while minimizing its destructive potential.

MULTIPLE LEADERS AND FOLLOWERS

A clarification is needed here.

The statement about how followership plays out in relation to the leader can be understood to assume there is only one leader at point zero, around which the circles of followership rotate. In reality, and particularly in political reality, there is always more than one leader, with concentric circles of followership around each. Consider, for example, the diffuse power centers in a federal system with national and regional political leadership. Or the power centers around each presidential or parliamentary cabinet member vying for resources for their department and potentially for their future opportunity to achieve higher office.

For the purposes of this book, we are focusing on the behaviors of each circle of followership around the *preeminent* political leader in a specific system. Similar dynamics simultaneously operate around other political leaders.

THE MANY FACES OF LEADING
AND FOLLOWING

We develop preferences and styles of leading and following within our family of origin, our culture, our school, and our work. The better the habits and principles we have developed about leading and following in other aspects of our lives, the better prepared we will be to play a meaningful and causal role in the political arena. How do we generally tend to follow those in authority?

- Do we follow without questioning? Or do we ask questions to understand the reason behind what we are asked or told to do?

- Do we "follow the herd," or do we pay attention to where the herd is going and the likely consequences of that?

- Do we regard leaders as parent figures who will take care of us, even save us? Or do we recognize them as other adults, hopefully trying to move things in a positive direction, who need our help and, at times, pushback?

Leading can come from the senior levels of an organized group or the lowest levels of a group. If one examines historical political dynamics, we see that most senior political leaders have a finger on the pulse of the populace and understand there are limits to what they, as leaders, can impose. In this sense, they are following those they lead.

The reverse is also true. At times, the most senior political leader has a benevolent or malevolent vision imposed on or sold to the citizenry. If they are effective in the art of communication and persuasion, the citizenry follows their lead, for better or worse.

Because they have a degree of control over the State's resources—its treasury, information and communication apparatus, and capacity for legal and armed enforcement—they have both persuasive and compulsory power. An entire range of dynamics emerges from this to the benefit or detriment of the citizenry they lead.

But we must not forget that, at times, the sheer power of numbers that the populace brings—citizens and noncitizens alike—and the willingness or refusal of that populace to follow the political leader, also has persuasive or coercive power. Think of historical figures who through succession, appointment, or orchestrated election been elevated to political heights and were later dismissed or overthrown by their subjects: to name just a few, King Louis XVI of France in 1792; Tsar Nicholas II of Russia in 1917; the shah of Iran in 1979; Ferdinand Marcos, the dictatorial president of the Philippines in 1986; Nicolae Ceaușescu, general secretary of the Romanian Communist Party in 1989; Hosni Mubarak, the dictatorial president of Egypt in 2011.

THE ENGAGED FOLLOWER

Contrary to cultural stereotypes, the *follower* does not play a passive role. It is an active role. Imagine partners dancing if the follower remained limp and the leader needed to drag them around the dance floor. This would not be a dance to watch or enjoy.

Political followership plays an active role. It requires alertness to whether leaders are trying their best to make things work as they should. Their efforts will always be less than perfect, but they still deserve support if they are generally pursuing the goals and values of the group.

In political systems, it is all too common for followers to become disillusioned and check out. Witness the low voter turnout in democracies that do not make voting mandatory or the cynicism toward the government. This is poor followership.

Mature followers recognize that the system of which they are part is always imperfect, and their leaders (like themselves) are imperfect. Yet, together, they can produce results that move the system in the direction of the common good. This is healthy, self-responsible followership.

If a political leader is seriously dysfunctional because of ineptness, corruption, ideology, or other factors, followers have the power to begin their own efforts to make things work better. Healthy political systems have a high level of citizen engagement to support existing leadership *or* provide alternative leadership options.

THE INFORMED FOLLOWER

Despite the prior view on follower engagement, engagement itself may or may not be beneficial. If we are not sufficiently informed, we are not prepared to make good choices. Those with questionable agendas can manipulate us. Now comes the hard part: How do we stay sufficiently informed to be responsibly engaged?

On any issue, at either end of the political spectrum, if we only get our information from one side of that issue or one end of the political spectrum, we cannot make an independent judgment. None of us have the time to become experts on the wide range of issues percolating in our political system at any given time. We need to rely on those who make their living deeply understanding the issues and candidates.

What we can do is consciously choose to get our information from several points on the political spectrum, then assess for ourselves which we judge to have greater value.

By diversifying the political information we receive and considering its accuracy and importance, we are internalizing the political process at the larger level of society: competing information and views are presented and debated before decisions are made. In a sense, we have become the political process on an individual level.

The task is now further complicated by the ease with which false information can be inserted into the system. Whole books can be, and undoubtedly are, written and repeatedly updated about how to navigate this well. For our purposes, it will need to be enough to consciously choose to find two or three sources of information with different perspectives. We can then build our own decisions from that process. Here's a vignette based on an actual occurrence.

Duke was confident he understood where things were at. He listened to his favorite talk show and talked with his friends, who also listened to it. They were downright mad at what they learned.

What they didn't think about was ratings. The talk show host kept his listener rating high, which drove his paid subscriptions and advertising fees. The more he riled up his listeners, the more they listened.

One day, the talk show host left his mic "hot," and Duke heard him say, "Those fools eat up anything I tell them." Duke's stomach turned.

He stopped "eating" there. Looking for a better information diet, he tried two or three other shows. None were satisfying on their own. He found, like a good balanced meal, it was more satisfying to listen in turn to each of them. He digested the different stories and the interpretations given to them and arrived at his own understanding of current developments. This sat well with his sense of himself as an independent thinker.

Wherever we are on the political spectrum, all of us would do well to avoid being force-fed a polarizing news diet from a single source. We may well be getting a mono diet without realizing it, as we feel ourselves in agreement and comfortable with what we are being told. It is up to us to recognize and insulate ourselves from mono diets, which may be indoctrination posing as news. This is a foundational awareness and practice of constructive political following.

Highly controlling regimes only want us to get information from one approved source. Why do this to ourselves when there is still available choice?

WHAT IS A POLITICAL CONTEXT?

What does it mean *to follow in a political context*?

Barbara Kellerman, a political scientist and scholar of leadership and followership, continually reminds us that there are three interacting elements: leadership, followership, and context.[1] Context greatly matters when considering the priorities of leaders and followers, affecting the appropriate and most effective styles to employ.

Let's examine how this broadly applies to a political context, understanding that, within this large category, specific context will also matter greatly.

The term *political* means different things to different people. There are organizational politics, group politics, even family politics. In this book, we examine the more formal systems that cultures develop to organize the communal lives of large numbers of people.

Several needs exist in all societies in one form or another. While not an exhaustive list, these include:

- The need to protect the people in that society from encroachment or aggression by neighboring societies

- The need for rules for how people within the society will act in relation to each other and their mutual rights

- The capacity to enforce those rules when necessary

- Providing members of society access to resources commensurate with the need to sustain and improve life

- Administration of large, cooperative projects that serve the public good, such as core infrastructure

- The availability and acceptance of a stable form of currency to facilitate exchanges of goods and services

- Managing the competition between subgroups that threatens the cohesion of society

When these basic functions of government are severely lacking, we have a failed state. Chaos ensues until a new governing solution emerges. Often, that solution is a strong political figure who can forcefully restore order. How they achieve the formal authority to do so can be a function of political competition or an extralegal act of seizing power. As this book focuses on interrupting and hopefully pre-venting the seizing of power, whether incrementally or in a violent spasm, let's start with an overview of ways to acquire the power to govern legitimately.

The political context of a society includes the customs, norms, and systems that society has developed for conferring the authority to govern and thereby provide the basic functions of government.

Different societies have developed significantly different ways of doing so, spanning from tribal councils to hereditary monarchs, to oligarchies of powerful families, to theocratic elders, to single ideological parties, to democratically elected representatives, with many variations in each of these and other models. Most of these systems seek to distribute power so it resides in more than one individual, even if some favor centralized authority more than others. This can take the form of multiple points of leadership with specialized jurisdiction and divided authority. Classically, this is the broad division of executive, legislative, and judicial authority.

The distribution of power can also be achieved by followers retaining certain powers of their own. An active citizenry makes its needs and preferences known, and advancing them is a requirement of the continued right to govern. A passive citizenry wakes up one morning and is surprised by a loss of rights.

While we may prefer to get on with our lives and not be burdened by the need to engage in political matters, sooner or later, the realities of political dynamics catch up with us and insist we pay attention. To retain a degree of agency, we become active participants in how our society is governed. Imagine reactions to a new government policy that limited the personal choices or freedoms of its citizens. It might sound something like this:

She couldn't be bothered with politics—it was either boring or nasty. There were so many more fun things to do in life. And there were things she wanted to achieve that required all her free time.

One day, she heard about legislation passed that would directly affect her ability to achieve those things. That

continued

wasn't fair! Who let that happen? Did she need to learn more about that and how to change it?

She was just one person. Could she really make a difference? It seemed she would need to try.

Political context has transformed her from a passive follower to one who is becoming actively engaged. Now, she would need to learn how to do so effectively.

With a baseline understanding of political followership and its responsibilities, let's turn to political leadership, its virtues, and its pitfalls.

CHAPTER 2

POLITICAL LEADERS

Uses and Abuses of Office

.

"Of all our passions and appetites, the love of power is of
the most imperious and unsociable nature since the pride
of one man requires the submission of the multitude."
—EDWARD GIBBON, *The Rise and Fall*
of the Roman Empire

STRONG LEADERS

Before we further examine the different types of political followers and how each can play its role effectively, we need to
set the stage by scrutinizing the leaders with whom they are
likely to engage.

Thousands of leadership development programs throughout the world tell us what ideal leadership is like and how
well-developed leaders should behave. In practice, few

political leaders conform to these ideals. They do not typically rise in political ranks based on taking leadership development programs. We need to understand how these leaders are likely to behave in practice.

There is great value in strong leadership. If you have worked for a weak leader who compromises on core values, is hesitant to make decisions, and vacillates based on every new perspective they hear, then you know firsthand the downsides of this poor leadership.

If you have worked for a strong leader focused on the group's goals, who upholds its values, gets important things done while taking care of their team members, seeks diversity of perspectives, and makes ethical decisions in tough situations, then you know the benefits of strong leadership.

An autocratic leader leads decisively—often without the finer points of healthy human relationships—but, at times, can be what a polity responds to or an organization seems to need. An example was Lee Kuan Yew, who led Singapore for thirty-one years. Under his autocratic leadership, he raised the city-nation from widespread poverty to one of the wealthiest countries in Asia with the lowest rate of corruption.

The price Singapore paid for this prosperity was an autocratic government that fiercely limited political freedoms and dissent. Due to the widely increased standard of living, Lee Kwan Yew's regime nevertheless enjoyed high approval ratings. However, the habit of autocratic rule persisted after his reign without his charisma and talent. Farah Stockman observed in the *New York Times*, "That's the thing about benevolent autocracies: They tend to expire. They either cease to be autocracies—as happened in South Korea and Chile—or they cease to be benevolent."[1]

The danger, as we will see, is that in the right context, with colluding followers, any strength autocratic leaders bring can soon become a liability if not balanced by courageous followers. At some point, unchecked autocratic leaders devolve into what we are calling *prototyrants*.

A prototyrant does not yet have unchecked power to inflict their will indiscriminately. They work aggressively to consolidate control over institutions that maintain and value their independence.

Strong leadership and prototyrannical leadership can initially appear similar in that they are decisive and move programs forward. But they come from fundamentally different perspectives on life—that all people deserve respect and have something to offer versus treating people as pawns in their egotistical pursuit of personal power.

How do these differences express themselves in social and political behavior?

COOPERATION AND COMPETITION

In nature, all things compete *and* cooperate. Look at any meadow or forest, and you will see the balance of these essential forces.

The same holds true in human endeavor. Success is most often realized through a balance of cooperation and competition. Leadership and followership strive for the dynamic interplay of these forces within the context in which they operate and the goals that propel them.

Competition and cooperation can be envisioned as a continuum. Optimally, they each are some distance from the extreme, at the point Aristotle called "the golden mean." Competition taken to the extreme of its side of the continuum becomes aggression and war. Cooperation taken to the extreme can become surrender and collusion.

When distinguishing between a prototyrant and a charismatic reformer, it is useful to look at their method of engagement. The dedicated reformer will remain strong in their interactions but not inflexible. They will not respond to criticism, warranted or otherwise, with unbridled attack. They will seek to explain their values and reasoning better while shrewdly strengthening support for their position.

The prototyrant will rarely if ever do this. They will meet criticism with an attack, verbal or otherwise. Think about this for a moment. Could you have a relationship with a friend or a family member whose only response to your requests for change was to attack you? Suppose you cannot envision sustaining a relationship on that basis. How do you imagine a political leader with this behavior can function in a system that distributes power and requires some degree of cooperation?

We all want political leaders who can't be "rolled," who can hold their own against tough political opponents and entrenched tyrants whose expansionist aims threaten our way of life. The failure of the thirty-second president of the United States, Franklin D. Roosevelt, to hold his own against the ruthlessness of the Soviet dictator Josef Stalin at the end of World War II arguably consigned tens of millions of Eastern Europeans to forty years of loss of basic freedoms.[2]

There is no question that authoritarian leadership can effectively meet the demands of certain situations. Criticism of this type of leadership is not based on a moral judgment or a claim that it lacks effectiveness. It can, in fact, be both moral and effective in a given context. The criticism is based on its typical—though not inevitable—trajectory toward dictatorial and tyrannical rule. It tends to move from competition to dominance and, in the extreme, to violence to achieve its aims. This is antithetical to a society committed to fundamental rules, rights, and freedom.

Followership that is coerced to support aggression or that does so out of a weak commitment to its ideals and a failure to mobilize its latent power, creates the conditions that support an emerging tyrant. The challenge for those who value cooperation is judging when to cooperate, when to compromise, and when to stand firm. When a point is approached that will doom the aggressive leader's overly competitive agenda, it is the followers' turn to lead and steer the dynamics toward an appropriate balance in whatever way our power permits.

As I wrote this, we were witnessing thousands of Israelis going into the streets to thwart the attempt to consolidate power in the office of the prime minister at the expense of an independent judicial system. Historical events continue to unfold, so we don't know the outcome of this action, though we do know it has already delayed the consolidation

continued

attempt. This is not to say there is no merit in the position of the prime minister, but in terms of balance, the society is correctly alarmed at the prospect of consolidating too much power in one office.

As often happens, between writing this and preparing the book for publication, other geopolitical events have overshadowed this particular resistance to the consolidation of power: the brutal conflict between the Palestinian group Hamas and the Israeli Defense Forces in Gaza. Nevertheless, it remains a cogent example of a cross section of society acting in the available political space to defend its institutions.[3]

Ideally, the leader will dial back their ferocity and champion the group's legitimate interests with healthy competitiveness—rather than seeking to annihilate opponents. Well-positioned followers can encourage this, but if not done skillfully, the leader may view the follower who counsels temperance as weak and disregard or replace them. The leader then creates an echo chamber in which the only sounds are those of their aggression amplified.

Regardless of short-term effectiveness, unremitting and uncompromising aggressiveness by the leader is a warning sign of an emerging tyrant. When reinforced by hardline followers with whom they surround themselves, it becomes the antithesis of the give-and-take required of leadership in a democratic process. To offset this runaway feedback loop— to pump the brakes—followers who seek to modulate the tyrannical trajectory must be strategic as well as courageous.

In the following chapters, we will examine obstacles to performing this balancing role at each degree of proximity to the leader and strategies for overcoming these obstacles.

If these efforts are successful, followers benefit from the competitive strength of the strong leader while containing the liabilities connected to their excesses. If they are unsuccessful, years may be spent under the scourge and devastation of tyrannical rule.

Adolph Hitler came within reach of dominating the world. He did this by signing a nonaggression pact on August 24, 1939, to cooperate with the Soviet Union in dividing up Europe. A week later, he invaded Poland, marking the official beginning of WWII. With the Soviet Union neutralized, Hitler was able to quickly conquer France and the small nations between the two countries and focus his military might on preparing to invade England.

The English heroically resisted, but their fate was still in question until Hitler, unable to contain his compulsion for dominance, broke the treaty and invaded Russia in June 1941. Historians generally agree this sealed Germany's fate, as it could not sustain a major two-front war once the United States entered on the side of England and its allies later that fateful year. Let us not forget that included in the tens of millions of people who lost their lives were millions of Germans who had elected and supported this compulsively aggressive leader.

CHARISMATIC LEADERS

The world needs effective political leaders, maybe even charismatic leaders. How on earth do you govern a country with hundreds of millions of people unless you can get their attention? And how do you get their attention unless you are larger than life, make equally large promises, and do things that compel attention?

This may go against the contemporary ideal in Western academia, which is that leadership should be inclusive and collaborative. I'm not arguing against this ideal in many situations. But how realistic is it on a national stage—not just in countries that have a history of liberal democracy but also in countries that have long histories of ruthless autocrats?

There are many global examples of countries that lack a strong leader or where an autocrat has been deposed, and the country descends into tribal fighting and civil war. It would seem there is virtue in a strong, even dominant, leader. But if we accept this, how do we draw the line between a strong leader—the strong leader the country needs to hold it together and keep it moving forward—and an autocratic leader with despotic tendencies who threatens to become a dictator, or worse, a tyrant?

The early twentieth-century sociologist Max Weber observed that in addition to traditional and legal authority, authority also appeared to emanate from the quality he called *charisma*. He offered this description of charisma: "[A] certain quality of an individual personality, by virtue of which he is set apart from ordinary men and treated as endowed with supernatural, superhuman, or at least specifically exceptional powers or qualities."[4]

A *certain quality* is a very vague definition, which eluded more precision. Perhaps this is one of those qualities you know when you see it. Once followers imbue a leader with this "exceptional" aura, they can be mesmerized and brought to believe that this leader alone has the ability to right the wrongs of the city, state, province, nation, or world. They become inured or willfully blind to any dangerous qualities the leader also displays that have the potential to wreak havoc on the checks and balances designed to restrain excesses of power.

Weber observed that this quality could not only sway large segments of the populace but was, at times, needed to overcome the calcification that can occur in large government bureaucracies. Once again, we have a quality that can be employed as a beneficial change agent but, when paired with autocratic tendencies, can bring millions under its sway to less beneficial outcomes. Followers at different levels of distance from the charismatic leader will need to use other characteristics or behaviors to judge if this is a leader to support and strengthen, a leader to monitor and check, or a leader whose further rise is best thwarted.

I was in Prague, Czech Republic, acting as a facilitator for a meeting where the country's former president, the poet and dissident Václav Havel, hosted a group of former heads of government and heads of state of democratic countries.

continued

Each participant had been a prime minister or president of their country. Several, like Havel, had been dissidents who succeeded autocratic or tyrannical leaders.

One evening, the group convened for a panel discussion with Havel; the recent president of Brazil, Fernando Henrique Cardoso; and former US President Bill Clinton. When Clinton entered the room, nearly all of the former dignitaries seemed to become electrified and rushed to swoon around Clinton, who fairly glowed in their midst. These men and women, who had risen to the highest positions in their own countries, were behaving like young fans at a rock concert.

BEYOND AUTHORITARIAN LEADERSHIP

We must think about these matters before we begin looking at the responsibilities of followers at different degrees of proximity to the leader. Otherwise, we will be prone to quickly label a strong leader, or even an able authoritarian leader, as a *dictator* or *prototyrant*. In its way, this tendency will also undermine the capacity of leaders to govern.

There are many scales of authoritarian personality traits. Displaying these traits alone does not make for dictatorial or tyrannical leadership. In certain contexts, authoritarian traits are an effective form of leadership, especially if the leader allows a deputy with more empathy to balance the harshness of the autocratic style. The danger is their transmuting, unbidden, into a dictatorial mode.

It is important to be precise when we use the term *dictator* in a political context. The *Encyclopedia Britannica* gives us historical background on the classical role of a dictator:

> Dictator, in the Roman Republic, a temporary magistrate with extraordinary powers, nominated by a consul on the recommendation of the Senate and confirmed by the Comitia Curiata (a popular assembly) . . . In Rome, dictators were resorted to only in times of military, and later internal, crises. The dictator's term was set at six months, although he customarily laid down his powers as soon as the crisis passed.

In contemporary government, we often use the Russian word *czar* to convey some of this meaning and these powers. Per the *Cambridge Dictionary*, *czar* designates "a person who has been given special powers by the government to deal with a particular matter." In the United States, for example, we refer to a "drug czar" overseeing drug policy issues.

The current meaning of the word *dictator* becomes less clear when we refer to national leaders who gain control of the levers of national power and aim to rule largely unchecked, though they cannot yet do so. I am referring to political leaders who seek to move into this phase as *prototyrants*. The distinction is that they have not been asked to assume these powers by elected representatives of the citizenry but have clawed power from other arms of government and usurped it for themselves. While they might use that power benignly, it is far more common to use their power extralegally and destructively. From there, it is not a large step to move from *dictator* to *tyrant* per the definition given in the introduction to this book—*an absolute ruler, unrestrained by law or constitution, who exercises absolute power oppressively and brutally.*

As you see, there is a continuum of behavior in those we refer to as "strong leaders." In practice, early in their power trajectories, we may be unable to differentiate between these leaders. Erring on the side of caution, we can assume that all strong leaders have *the potential* to become dictatorial or tyrannical given the right context. If that is so, we must find the balance between supporting them and preemptively constraining them.

Constitutions, like those of the United States or other countries, attempt this to their credit. The reality is that those only constrain the autocrat during relatively normal times. As soon as a crisis threatens the fabric of a country or can be made to seem to threaten the fabric of a country, there are great temptations to override the constitution and any checks on power.

One of the ways that contemporary autocrats attempt to mask their transition to dictatorial control is by amending or rewriting a constitution to weaken checks on their power. It looks like a legitimate process but shifts power away from the legislature, courts, a free press, and civil society organizations in ways that consolidate their own hold on the levers of governing.

A political scholar on constitutional changes offers many examples of this tactic, including the maneuver by Turkish President Recep Tayyip Erdoğan. In 2017, he introduced a package of eighteen amendments in a referendum, a vehicle that can be worded to obfuscate its consequences. Richard Albert of the University of Texas in Austin estimates this effectively diluted about 40 percent of the constitution, weakening the checks on Erdoğan's power and making it possible for him to rule for an additional sixteen years. This has reinforced concerns about a trajectory toward dictatorship in a country that is an important member of NATO.[5]

If the rules as they exist thwart the consolidation of power, the prototyrant will focus on rewriting or ripping up the rules. In many countries, amending or scrapping a constitution is not as arduous as in the United States. In the United States, precisely because the process is so arduous, the prototyrant is more likely to find ways of reinterpreting existing rules in favor of their aggregating power.

To provide constraints, we need a culture of active followership that continuously discerns between leaders and their acts—which of those acts should be supported and which should be questioned or thwarted? Which, despite any short-term benefits, are outweighed by the long-term risk they pose in the hands of this political leader or their successors?

That's an exhausting way to live, isn't it? Yes. But fire and safety drills in high-risk environments also consume our resources. Yet these must be done. The question is how to do this effectively at different levels of society while we get on with our lives?

CONSOLIDATING POWER

All new regimes seek to gain control of the levers of power within their formal and informal governing systems. Similarly to distinguishing prosocial and anti-social populists, we are pressed to differentiate appropriate consolidation of power from that which is dangerous. The matter is made more difficult as the amount of power needed and how it is acquired and distributed is once again related to the context of the system of governance and events occurring within and outside it.

In the trajectory of a prototyrant, other formal institutions like the legislature, courts, and civil service, and informal institutions like political parties, the media, and nongovernmental organizations will be targeted to be brought under the autocrat's control, or weakened and eliminated. Counterintuitively, the autocrat may expand some of these institutions, though packing them with loyalists under his control. This can lend an apparency of legitimacy to the regime while simultaneously bringing potential competitors under the prototyrant's distrustful eye.

What will need watching is how subservient these institutions become to the prototyrant instead of remaining committed to their legitimate public mission. Discerning this will require vigilance on the part of activists, the bureaucracy, and the media. Interrupting the creation of a monopoly on governing power, which nearly always leads to the misuse and abuse of power, will require multiple acts of courageous followership.

Let's look at the distinctions between strong and tyrannical leadership and then examine two historical examples to get a clear sense of what is meant by a prototyrant consolidating power versus a strong leader creating the conditions for successful governing.

STRONG VS. TYRANNICAL LEADERSHIP

Until a condition is named, it is nearly impossible to identify or manage it. Naming must be sufficiently precise to place what is being named in the general context to which it belongs and differentiate it from similar members of that class. This is certainly true of political leadership.

Political leadership can be described as a class of people governing a large, organized body of individuals and communities with common needs for public safety and welfare. At the same time, the term is so broad that it could include a wide range of historic figures such as Nelson Mandela, Abraham Lincoln, Margaret Thatcher, Indira Gandhi, Josef Stalin, and Chairman Mao Ze Dong.

There is a spectrum of political leadership, from positive leadership at one end to tyrannical behavior at the other. In reality, neither form exists in purity. Therefore, we need to be astute in understanding the progression from true leadership to destructive, tyrannical behavior.

It will serve us well to get better at perceiving the telltale signs of leadership morphing into tyranny. Along the way, embryonic tyrannical behavior seems to serve and protect the interests of its followers. Perhaps in very small doses, it does. How do we determine when those small doses are beginning to metastasize and must be excised before they are unstoppable?

This is a typical progression toward tyrannical behavior:

- Political observer—limited influence

- Populist candidate—striving for power

- Officeholder—achieving power (legally or extralegally)

- Governing officer—using legitimate powers of office

- Authoritarian officeholder—using and, at times, abusing power

- Dictatorial powers (emergency-based)—unilaterally using specified powers

- Dictatorial powers (usurped and entrenching)— unilaterally using/abusing general powers

- Dictatorial powers (consolidated)—exercising supreme power beyond questioning

- Tyrant (arbitrary, unconstrained, cruel abuse of power)—rule by terror

Think of the progression of Vladimir Putin, at this writing the tyrannical ruler of Russia. He has been president or prime minister of Russia since 1999—nearly a quarter of a century and counting. His progression to tyrant deviates somewhat from our model in the early part of his career when he served in political staff rather than elected positions, but maps closely to it in recent years. After serving sixteen years as an intelligence officer, his political career began in 1991 as an aide in the office of the mayor of St. Petersburg. After five years of learning the ropes and earning whatever favors his successive positions allowed, he relocated to Moscow.

In Moscow, he continued working his way through increasingly influential appointed positions and joined the administration of Boris Yeltsin, Russia's first democratically elected president. Winning Yeltsin's trust, he went through a further series of appointments that culminated in becoming Russia's fifth prime minister in less than two years. From here, it was a legal step to acting president when Yeltsin resigned and then to presidential candidate.

In his first term as president, Putin struggled to manage crises and retain a positive approval rating. When speaking as a guest to the German parliament in 2001, he claimed "democratic rights and freedom" as the "key goal of Russia's domestic policy."[6]

In the ensuing years, despite these claims, and with an improving economy giving him cover, he methodically consolidated power, replacing elected governors of Russia's provinces with appointed lackeys, weakening the power of the legislature (the *duma*) or the independence of the courts to serve as checks on his power, while beginning a de facto policy of assassinating media critics and political rivals.

These courageous souls tried to interrupt his consolidation of power. Their failure to do so exemplifies the risks of being unable to create a supportive coalition in the politically available window when the economic and social context is more favorable to the autocrat.

Twenty years after his ascension to power as a purported democrat, he justified the unprovoked invasion of sovereign Ukraine when it met fierce resistance with these chilling words: True Russians would "spit them out like a gnat that accidentally flew into their mouths" and achieve "a necessary self-purification of society."[7]

Observers who met with Putin early in his presidency and years later observed the changes that unchallenged power was working in him. Condoleezza Rice, former secretary of state to President George W. Bush and fluent Russian speaker observed: "When I first met him, you had to lean in a little to understand what he was saying. I've seen Putin go from a little shy, to pretty shy, to arrogant and now megalomaniacal."[8]

Look how that tracks with the progression to political tyrant.

In contrast to the trajectory of a Putin, a strong leader without dictatorial ambition will act to win the cooperation of other critical elements of the political system. When they cannot, they will take legal steps to implement their reformist agenda in the face of opposition. They may push the boundaries of acceptable power moves, but the boundaries are still recognizable. A positive example of this in twentieth-century European history is the requirement for greater centralized power, which Charles de Gaulle placed prior to accepting the French presidency in 1958.

Through talent, ambition, wile, resoluteness, and

self-promotion, De Gaulle was viewed as the hero of the French Resistance during WWII, when Germany occupied France. In 1944, upon the liberation of France, he became head of the provisional government until 1946, when, dissatisfied with the inadequate powers imbued in the executive branch, he retired from public life. In 1958, in the throes of crisis, the National Assembly invited him back to assume the presidency of France during what is known as the Fourth Republic. Power still largely resided in an unstable parliamentary system. De Gaulle insisted on constitutional revisions that gave the office of the president sufficient power to govern stably. The new constitution was approved by referendum, and he was elected president of the Fifth Republic later that year by a wide margin, holding the office for eleven years. During this time, he also recognized Algeria's independence, ending France's antidemocratic colonial rule of Algeria.[9]

What distinguishes this example from the acts of a prototyrant is that the new French constitution clearly preserved adequate checks and balances on presidential power. In 1969, he held a referendum that, perhaps surprisingly, proposed greater *decentralization* of power. After losing the referendum, he resigned later that year. De Gaulle had the larger-than-life presence and dramatic, even bullying, behavior of a potential dictator but did not use his moment in the limelight to undermine the institutions of his country's democratic government.

The key takeaway from this chapter is distinguishing between the appropriate power a political leader needs to serve well and their push for excessive power that eliminates any checks on their behavior. There may be disagreement on where exactly that line lies, but when a threshold is being approached there should not be avoidance of seeing a pattern emerging. That is the crucial window for interrupting the trajectory—for applying the available braking mechanisms—before the pattern becomes entrenched and unassailable.

CHAPTER 3

CIRCLES OF FOLLOWERS

The Political Leadership They Create

.

"If I had to reduce the responsibilities of a good follower to a single rule, it would be to speak truth to power."
—WARREN BENNIS, founding chair, The Leadership Institute, University of Southern California

---

Much has been studied and written about followership since Robert Kelley published his article in the *Harvard Business Review*, "In Praise of Followers," and his book *The Power of Followership*, and since I published my first book, *The Courageous Follower*, more than a quarter century ago.

Nevertheless, simply talking about the dichotomy and relationship of leaders and followers is insufficient to understand and possibly improve the dynamics within political spheres that are crucial to the well-being of humanity.

NOT ALL LEADERS OR FOLLOWERS
ARE CREATED EQUAL
A Model of Followership
By distance from the political leader

Circle 5—The populace or citizenry who support or reject the leadership

Circle 4—Activists who create support or opposition

Circle 3—Bureaucrats who execute or thwart policies

Circle 2—Elites who stand to gain or lose privilege

Circle 1—Confidants who intensify or modulate ambitions and style

There are leaders at the apex of their national government and leaders at many levels below, all with certain responsibilities and powers. There are followers at every level of this hierarchy, from those surrounding the supreme leader to those surrounding and working with leaders at each level.

In the political arena, there are followers who are not present in the room but potentially have the ultimate power of taking to the streets and social media platforms to question, challenge, elect, un-elect, defeat, or even overthrow political leaders. The following sections are an overview of the different powers, vulnerabilities, challenges, and responsibilities at each of these levels of leading and following.

The Prototyrant's Formula and Circles of Followers

When we examine history, we can discern that there is almost a formula for how a rising tyrant acts toward the different circles of followers. Undoubtedly, it is inexact and varies, given each specific context, but the shape is familiar. It is useful to identify this, as doing so will also identify the challenges facing each circle of followers and the options for them to resist collusion. Let's start with the outer circle, which will also be called the Fifth Circle.

Fifth Circle: The Populace. As I have mentioned earlier, while *citizenry* is the more common term, *populace* is more inclusive, as it embraces everyone living within the realm of the government and its laws, rules, and services. This is the circle of followers with the least individual contact with the authoritarian leader. Their power is latent. Collectively, it may support the rise of a leader with autocratic tendencies and eventually overthrow them.

The rising tyrant's strategy for this circle is to promise them the world and, while resources last, make their lives easier with price controls, benefits not previously accessible to them, and permission to take wealth from those labeled "enemies of the State." All the while, the prototyrant showers them with an überpatriotic message that puts them at the center of their world, conferring a sense of recognition that life had not previously granted them. The strategy includes dazzling the populace with symbols of the regime that champions them and narratives that tie their present and future to a glorious, if mythical, past.

If the hopes of this circle are sufficiently raised, they become enthusiastic, conformist followers who go along with and even drive the program. After the tyrant's corruption and bellicosity bankrupt the nation, the true cost of their support is felt in bread lines, lost kinfolk, and ruined dreams of a better life. As often as not, these latter stages lead to revolt and overthrow of the tyrant. This also opens the path for the next tyrant to emerge using similar early strategies or unremitting brute force.

Fourth Circle: Activists and Organizers. This circle divides into those messianically supporting the rising tyrant as a savior of the people and those who see the inevitable dire results of their ascension and actively oppose them.

Those who passionately support the rising tyrant are rewarded with perks the regime can command and the promise of promotion within the regime's ranks. They become colluders.

Those opposing the rising tyrant are correctly viewed as most dangerous to their success. If they can wake the populace to the looming trajectory, they threaten to end the authoritarian's project before they accrue the power required to rule absolutely. The autocrat's tactic for the opposing group is intimidation by every means possible—undermine their reputation, their livelihood, their communication platforms, and, if that is insufficient, threaten, beat, imprison, or murder them.

The true colors of the ascending tyrant show first toward this circle of strong-minded individuals who either collude and follow fanatically or courageously resist and oppose the dangerous rise.

Third Circle: Bureaucrats. Those who keep the government functioning. Max Weber wrote extensively about bureaucracy as the most efficient means of achieving the implementation of the sovereign's policies. On the positive side, rules govern decisions that can be made by professional staff—the bureaucrats—eliminating the favoritism and whimsy of earlier systems of organization.

While espousing the virtues of the system, including its efficiencies, Weber also saw the vices: the elimination of human judgment and personal accountability in decision-making.[1] Later, sociologists observed that once the individual is no longer morally accountable, they focus on technical perfection, which at its worst leads to the extremes of better ways to implement repressive or genocidal policies.

The autocrat counts on the bureaucratic culture to do his bidding and dirty work: to be conformist followers. The autocrat installs political enforcers (colluder followers) in key positions to transmit their intentions deep into the bureaucratic machinery. They seek to weaken civil service protections so this marginally privileged class will be frightened of losing the livelihoods that keep them from falling into the anxiety or desperation experienced by those without secure incomes and benefits. The autocrat is caught off guard when rare individuals transcend the culture and take moral stands in courageous opposition to destructive programs and orders.

Second Circle: Elites. Historically, a prototyrant cannot amass the power needed to fulfill their tyrannical ambitions without help. They require at least tacit support, if not active collusion, from a segment of elites in the society.

The clever prototyrant positions themselves as the best hope for maintaining the elites' highly privileged lifestyle with policies that favor their economic interests. In the short term, elites often thrive on a kleptocratic culture and vast expenditures on militaristic expansion. In their hubris, they are confident they can control this thug to serve their interests. They are confounded when they wake up one morning to find it is the tyrant who now controls them.

As the prototyrant consolidates power, they target a particularly high-profile elite or a potential rival. making of them a cautionary example to others by throwing this once-exalted mogul into prison and stripping his family of their wealth. Those with the resources and connections to flee the country often do so, leaving a larger power vacuum for the tyrant to fill with their cowed cronies.

First Circle: Confidants. As prototyrants turn on or alienate elites who have the power to oppose them, their sense of personal danger grows. They have systematically turned once-powerful supporters into resentful potential enemies. Their inner circle becomes ever more important as the pool shrinks of those they can trust.

Inner circle members are tightly bound to the prototyrant, partly by familial connection and partly by a long history of helping their ascension. With rare exceptions, they are all-in colluders and are amply rewarded psychologically by intimate access to the supreme leader. They may also be materially rewarded with wealth from "sweetheart" contracts or clandestine payments in exchange for the use of their access. But even these may be insufficient to guarantee their loyalty.

The increasingly paranoid prototyrant binds the inner circle more closely to him by involving confidants in his corruption and crimes. If he is brought down, they will be brought down. If he is found guilty of crimes against humanity, he makes sure they will also have blood on their hands, ensuring they will stand with him to the end. The reward for their loyalty is the trap sprung to preclude escape from the nightmarish regime they have enabled. These grim patterns have occurred repeatedly in history.

Now that you know the lures, traps, and vulnerabilities of each circle of followers, we will further dissect their role vis-à-vis the emerging tyrant and examine the early awareness needed to avoid being snared and the strategies available to interrupt and possibly transform the toxic progression.

A Bird's Eye View

Were we to use this lens of five circles of followers at any number of massive rallies that eventually emerge against strongman rule, we might find those assembled fitting into these striations:

The people in the street looked at their vast numbers, which gave them a sense of power. Pent-up resentments were, at last, finding an outlet.

continued

They were unaware that among them were activists who had employed the techniques of their playbook to fire them up and get them to leave their everyday lives long enough to register their collective outrage and demand for change. On the other side of the street, activists were doing the same for the crowd they had summoned in support of the charismatic populist's actions.

The crowds began to notice the increasing presence of police and soldiers in riot gear. One of these security personnel looked back at the crowds and wondered why he was there. They were his people. Would he need to attack those opposing the president? The thought disturbed him, but the five children at home needed the food his paycheck bought every month.

A prominent media host entered the crowd, finding space for her cameraman. This was sure to get great ratings on the evening news, though she had to be careful not to appear sympathetic to the opposition.

From a balcony, the president's son watched the growing throngs and realized he would need to recommend his father make significant conciliatory gestures or flee the country before he disastrously used his emergency powers to order the security forces to fire on the crowd.

From this overview, you have gotten a sense of where you fit into the follower schema in relation to the primary political leader. You may also fit into additional circles for other leaders with whom you work. For example, you may be a confidant for a mid-level elected official but an activist for a national political candidate on your own time. As we drop into a more extensive examination of each circle, you will see which points relate to you personally while creating a better map of the leader-follower system of which you are a part.

CHAPTER 4

THE POPULACE CIRCLE

You and the Foundation of Political Power

.

"The greatest power is not money power,
but political power."
—WALTER ANNENBERG,
philanthropist and US ambassador

- Circle 5 Populace
- Circle 4 Activists
- Circle 3 Bureaucrats
- Circle 2 Elites
- Circle 1 Confidants

LEADER

Inner Circle
Near Inner Circle
Middle Circle
Near Outer Circle
Outer Circle

**If you are a citizen of your country, you are a part of
the populace.** If you are not a citizen but circumstances
have made this the country where you live, you are another

part of the populace. Citizens and noncitizens alike are impacted by the government under whose authority they find themselves.

We may not be fond of that government and its leaders. We may not consider ourselves a follower of the leaders who currently exercise political authority. But our lives are affected by their decisions and actions. We will need to choose the degree of support we give those leaders, the degree to which we try to avoid their impact on our lives, or the degree to which we will work to elevate different leaders.

The word populace comes from *polis*, the Greek word for *city*, and is related to *polity*, a society organized under some form of government, and to *politics*, the activities associated with governance. The *populist* leader plays into our needs as members of this community, typically inflating what they can do for us.

We may belong to one of the other four circles of followers that overlap with this identity and go beyond it. We may be a noncitizen activist. We may need to be a citizen to serve as we do in the government. We may be a well-heeled émigré applying for citizenship while finding ways to support political candidates. We may be the mayor or governor or president's son or daughter.

In these roles, we are also part of the polity we call our city, state, country, and home. We are the people who the government is there to serve.

In this chapter, we look at what it means to be a follower of a political leader whom we see and hear but probably never personally meet. We may see them at a rally. More often, we see them through media and get to "know them" through the perspectives of other people who may or may not ever meet them.

Yet, they are the leader!

Suppose the leader is charismatic and casts their "spell" on us. How do we maintain the independent judgment needed to support them while being alert to any tendency on their part to misuse or abuse power?

You will notice I am asking a question about us, not them. *How do* we *maintain independent judgment?*

I keep turning the lens back on us, as it is ourselves over whom we have the most potential influence. What are *we* doing in relation to political power, and what might *we* do differently?

BORING POLITICAL LEADERS

As members of the polity, oddly enough, when we feel somewhat tepid about our political leaders, it generally means they are doing a reasonably good job with the basic functions of governing. If we neither regard them enthusiastically as saviors nor worryingly as menaces. we are likely to be living in fairly stable times. We can get on with our lives and depend on the government for its basic, legitimate services—safety, lawfulness, infrastructure, the stability on which economic life depends, and social services if other institutions in our culture do not provide for these.

There are always communal challenges, of course, and some reason to be less-than-fully satisfied with political leadership, whether at a local, regional, or national level. But in "good times," these do not rise to the top of our concerns.

Enjoy these times, as they never last.

Sooner or later, major issues arise that drastically affect the community, the region, the nation. Some even threaten their very existence: lack of water in an arid region. Food shortage due to crop failures. Chaos in financial markets. Pandemics, wars, natural disasters, massive technological, energy, or supply chain disruptions.

Hopefully, in the interludes between crises, the government will predict and prepare for how to meet the next wave of challenges. But we don't feel the need to pay close attention, whether or not we should. It is not that we don't care about political leadership. It just doesn't seem that pressing at the moment. This is a good time to begin paying more attention—*before* times change and catch us off guard.

GOVERNMENT OFTEN WORKS BETTER THAN IT IS GIVEN CREDIT FOR

It never ceases to amaze me that we can walk down the street of a major city like New York and see tens of thousands of people rushing by, not harming each other, following the basic etiquette of crossing streets and stopping at red lights, selling and buying a myriad of goods with a stable currency, using public transportation, and so forth. None of this makes news, as it is largely working!

It is when times feel threatening that we look for leadership to rally around, leadership that has strong, even messianic, qualities. Crime on public transportation or in the streets may be on the rise, garbage may be piling up due to work stoppages, a pandemic may be straining basic services, solutions to homelessness are slow in coming. These are more dangerous times as we seek out larger-than-life leaders with all the potential for greatness or malignancy they bring with them. These are times when we must pay attention to what type of leaders we, as followers, are calling into existence.

As citizens, I believe it is healthy to recognize how the government is functioning overall, despite deficiencies that must be addressed. This proofs us against ambitious candidates who want us to believe things are catastrophic and that only they can correct them. We know, historically, where this line of thinking has led. Meanwhile, if we are living in reasonable social conditions, we need to keep the criticisms we have of the government in perspective.

A satisfaction survey was done in the town of Blissville. It found that citizens were disturbed by the poor state of the rosebushes and other plantings in the town square. They were quite disappointed about the government's neglect of their park.

The mayor was thrilled with these results. Why?

There were almost no complaints about the sewer system, the crime rate, the economy, the schools, or transportation. Government was working. Now, the mayor could focus on improving the park.[1]

I encourage each of us to establish our authentic baseline of appreciation for government. Look around for a moment and notice all the basic things that, to a large degree, are working. From there, we can focus on the things that do need improvement and how to realistically make those happen, without would-be political saviors.

WHEN GOVERNMENT REALLY ISN'T WORKING

It's rarely the case that government doesn't work at all and becomes a failed state, though often, it works much better for some than for others. Those "others" are usually found in the general populace, not among the legions of bureaucrats or the fortunate elites.

In states that are teetering on failing, many in the populace feel desperate. In its extreme, what we think of as *law and order* has broken down. Official corruption and gang violence make life unsafe. Money has ceased to hold value. Food becomes scarce. From this very real sense of desperation, an archetypal hero is wished for and sought. When one seems to appear, there is cautious relief that maybe life will get better.

In this situation, personal safety and reassurance that one's family can be fed, sons won't be dragged into a gang or a corrupt military, daughters will be respected, and jobs can be found, take precedence over the finer points of democracy and civil rights. This, of course, is the fertile soil in which prototyrants arise.

There may indeed be a situation in which a tough auto-cratic leader is needed to reestablish a sense of order. The populace may be willing to give them a large degree of dicta-torial power if they will only turn around the situation that is making life extremely difficult. The leader may succeed suffi-ciently for the populace to be supportive of them, despite the loss of certain rights and freedoms.

At the time of this writing, we have a classic example play-ing out in the Central American country of El Salvador. The country has been plagued by vicious gang violence. Eighty murders in one weekend demanded action from the government. In a country of 6.5 million people, the president of El Salvador, Nayib Bukele, incarcerated over 73,000 men suspected of gang complicity. At times, his means have been extralegal, but they are not reported to include extralegal killings like those done by Rodrigo Duterte, president of the Philippines from 2016 to 2022. Though, inevitably, some of those arrested were not guilty, any injustice can be reversed. President Bukele's approval rating soared to a stratospheric 90 percent. Imagine no lon-ger having to worry that your sons will be coerced into gangs or your daughters will be attacked on their way to buy bread. People were desperate for a sense of safety and stability, and this dictatorial approach gave that to them. Bukele is seeking a second term and has signaled that he will end the state of emergency, which has allowed him to take extraordinary measures.[2]

But the populace must be wary. The taste of such power, for many men, is difficult to relinquish. Instead of riding into the sunset like a Hollywood hero, they begin entrenching themselves for the long haul. The slippery slope from autocrat to dictator to tyrant begins.

If the slide down that slope continues, there is still a window of opportunity to interrupt the descent. It will require sufficient members of the populace to maintain awareness of where the trajectory is leading, supporting the leader's virtues and decrying their excesses. The same resolve they showed in supporting the "new sheriff in town" will now be needed to hold him in check so he does not become the new mafioso don.

A populace committed to good public safety and good government can do both. The Roman example is relevant. Give the strongman six months to clean up the streets. Give him another six months if needed. If he claims the state of emergency must continue indefinitely, he is at the threshold that lies between the dictator and the tyrant. It is time to raise the alarm. What might a protest sign read?

THE STATE OF EMERGENCY IS OUR NEXT EMERGENCY

BELONGING TO SOMETHING LARGER

While we love our independence, humans also want to belong to something larger than ourselves. Doing so is energizing and often a high point of life. Sometimes, the way we do this is fleeting, like being at a thrilling sporting event. Sometimes, it is lifelong, like being an avid supporter of our home team in their glory or defeat. Sometimes, it is complex—a social, religious, or political movement doing important work in the world.

We will focus here on the political.

From a cynical view, *politics* has come to sound like something smarmy and untrustworthy. Yet *politics* is the container of our communal lives. Our politics determine the type of nation in which we will live, raise our children, follow our dreams, and, hopefully, not have them crushed by our government or a hostile invader.

Being part of mass political support for a leader or movement usually begins with simple concerns about the quality of our lives or with the encouragement of others we trust. It progresses to our strong belief in the leader and their agenda.

Just as we love our sports heroes and our entertainment idols, we can be excited by our political superstars. But the consequences are much more serious. We give our political sovereign the power of the state. This always includes the power of life and death. We must never forget that this is what we are conferring.

There are many people who have experienced the excitement of supporting movements for greater freedom, autonomy, and justice, even religious ecstasy. These elevate a real or symbolic leader who passionately represents the ideals they come to hold as their own. Regrettably, there are just as many who have experienced this adulation in support of movements and leaders that ultimately proved destructive to them and millions of others.

We would be well served by keeping a little reality checker on our shoulder. Don't let it spoil the excitement of being part of a movement greater than ourselves, but have it whisper in our ear: *Am I getting carried away? Am I still asking good questions? Am I putting this human being on too high a pedestal?*

BIG VISION

People like leaders with a large vision of what is possible, especially if the leader's story offers them hope for personal relevance in the world—more so if it offers the prospect of a better world, even if that is more wishfulness than reality.

Most of us derive meaning in life from our close circle of family and friends, the work we do, and the community to which we contribute. But there is also a longing to rise above the mundane, to live more expansively. This holds true from the bottom to the top of society. At the bottom, it may take the form of playing the lottery against all odds of winning. At the top, it may result in susceptibility to wild investment schemes that have little basis in reality.

This creates a challenge for followers with larger-than-life leaders who promise us a much better future. We do not want to discount them. At times, they make a fundamental and positive difference in the lives of many. At the same time, the correct stance is to remember their human fallibility. Stay alert for how power may begin to distort their service to the groups they are leading.

This is particularly true with political leaders and the services we need them to render. We cannot expect perfection from them. By its very nature, non-autocratic political leadership requires compromise and sometimes uncomfortable arrangements with unusual political allies: the "strange bedfellows" effect. Both Republicans and Democrats raised their eyebrows when they heard that Republican financier and activist Charles Koch, of the Koch brothers, and Democratic President Obama collaborated to pass large criminal justice system reform legislation.[3]

As political followers, we need to cut leaders slack while staying vigilant for fundamental betrayals of core values. When these are detected, we must be alert for the leader using their persuasive skills to make us believe there is nothing to be concerned about. There is.

It can be hard to acknowledge this. At last, we thought we had a champion. Yet the fate of your generation—whether it will see progress for you and those you love or whether it will be mired in conflict and struggles for personal freedom—depends on distinguishing a leader with a great, positive vision from one who talks a good game while dismantling the hard-won safeguards of those freedoms. What you think, say, and do about this will influence those around you.

We must do our best to see through the image-making machine for the emerging realities, overcome our reluctance to see these signals and use the open window of opportunity to question them.

THE POLITICAL LEADER'S MACHINE AND OUR MIND

All we have through which to view our world is our mind. This is so fundamental that we forget our mind is mediating our experience of reality. We are the proverbial fish who do not realize they are swimming in the water, as where else could they swim?

The framework that has been instilled or developed in our mind influences how we see reality, indeed what we see as reality. When we see a long gun, are we seeing a weapon of war or an instrument of individual rights? This requires us to examine and, at times, protect ourselves from the narrative others seek to establish in our minds. And others are always attempting to do so.

Political candidates and officeholders build message machines to grab our attention and put it where they want, away from hard questions they wish to avoid. We hear the spokespersons for the political leader all saying more or less the same thing, using the same buzzwords across many media platforms. They are working to create a narrative in our mind, whether that is a benign or dangerous one.

The leader who is self-aggrandizing works overtime to populate our minds with the burnished narrative they wish us to hold of them. We need to maintain a healthy distance from which we can view and make our own decisions about the leader's data, claims, thinking, actions, and character.

Asking ourselves a few basic questions can help us retain our perspective. The answers are less important than developing the habit of questioning.

- *What is the narrative the leader's machine is selling us?*

- *What about it seems true? What seems questionable? Why?*

- *If we are honest with ourselves, do we have doubts about the message or the leader?*

- *What are our concerns about them?*

WHAT WE BELIEVE

Seeing the different potential in movements and leaders, for good or harm, begins with seeing ourselves as clearly as possible.

When we form an attachment to a leader, it has a certain stickiness—our image of them, once formed, tends to stick. Yet few of us or our leaders remain static. As time and events progress, when we look at the leader, do we notice differences cropping up in them or our evaluation of them? This may be more difficult than it seems. At any given point, two individuals look at the same data and come to opposite interpretations.

However, we arrive at our interpretation, once we come to believe something, regardless of its truth or error, we tend to continue to believe that. New information we receive will seem to support it. We reflexively classify information that contradicts our belief as false, suspect, or unimportant. Who has the time and energy to continuously question ourselves? That would exhaust us, even paralyze us.

This tendency to adhere to a position once we pick it is a fundamental trap of which to be aware. That we currently believe something does not necessarily make it continue to be true. And it does not make the contradictory information we receive false.

As a citizen, as a follower of a leader or political faction, at some point we need to ask ourselves:

- *When did we first form a particular belief?*

- *On what basis, or because of whom, did we come to believe it?*

- *Are we open to examining our beliefs to determine whether giving our support is still the right thing?*

I'm not suggesting we become skeptics, doubting and questioning everything. I am suggesting we need to stay alert to our *resistance* to letting in new or contrary information—catch ourselves in the act and become curious enough to examine contradictions.

This is true in life generally. In political life, this is particularly important. Passions run high. A lot is at stake: the power to set a course for a whole nation, to choose winners and losers, to take care of one's friends, and neutralize one's opponents. Each side spins stories that credit themselves and discredit the other. We find ourselves leaning into and identifying with one of the narratives. There's a comfort in knowing what it is we believe and support and what we don't. We feel righteous about our beliefs!

But are they true?

What we eventually come to believe is not as important as periodically examining what we already believe, how we came to believe it, what keeps us believing it, and whether it is time to question those beliefs. That way, we control them rather than our beliefs controlling us.

Doing this requires conscious effort. Inertia is on the side of our current thinking.

Growing up, Derek Black had little doubt about what his future as an adult held. He was determined to carry on the work his parents, Chloe and Don (founder of the white nationalist website Stormfront), had spent decades devoting their lives to promoting the idea that the US should be purged of all non-white races.

At ten, while growing up in West Palm Beach, Florida, he started his Stormfront offshoot for kids. By the time he turned twenty, he had his daily radio show on a local station where listeners could tune in and listen as he spouted the group's racist philosophy.

However, life as Black knew it took a dramatic change shortly after he began studying German and medieval history at New College of Florida in 2010. He kept a low profile during his first semester, never discussing his beliefs and trying to fit in with the other ethnically diverse students, but was eventually outed as being the poster

continued

boy for white nationalism. He immediately found himself shunned and harassed by nearly everyone on the famously liberal campus.

Then came the dinner invitation from Matthew Stevenson, the college's only Orthodox Jew, who held Shabbat dinners in his dorm room on Friday nights.

Black began to realize that the evidence he'd always used to support his racist views—involving supposed IQ differences between the races and immigrant crime rates—had been fabricated, inflated, or misused by those in his movement.

Black renounced his former white nationalist position in an open letter that his father initially thought was a forgery. It was not. Black and Stevenson went on to share their story with the world. It is really a dual story, both important: Stevenson's was a story of resisting peer pressure to shun Derek Black and inviting him to his table to create a relationship that transcended ideology. Black's was the story of a courageous person reexamining their beliefs and forming a new sense of identity based on a truer picture of the world.[4]

CULTURE IS DEEPLY INGRAINED

Why is it so hard to question and reassess our views? To follow a leader while retaining a sense of independent thinking and accountability?

The culture of society is so deeply ingrained that it typically needs no enforcement. It lives and operates within us.

If this is a culture that celebrates individuality, diversity, and mutual care, this is a happy state of affairs. If this is a culture that values conformity and obedience above all else, it also seeps in deeply. It is self-regulating and only occasionally needs to be externally enforced.

The culture is the context of our individual life, our communal life, and our future—all in one. It is against our immediate interest to think about it differently, to question it, speak against it, or fail to reinforce it in others. But is it in our long-term interest?

Both leaders and followers are learners. Learners develop their mental models of the real world from their perceptions of that world. Much of that learning comes from family and peers and is mediated through their culture, which becomes ours, too. The subsets of our culture give us our sense of identity. Who are we within the broader landscape of a whole country, region, or nation? We need to anchor ourselves within these groups. This confers a crucial sense of belonging.

"We're a military family."

"We're a union family."

"We're a Christian family."

"We've been farmers for six generations."

"We're immigrants who need to fit in."

Each group tends to have a political leaning that aligns with its values. It favors candidates who seem committed to protecting those values. This is useful, up to a point. If we are so attached to that identity and political viewpoint that we cannot also identify with the broader nation of which we are a part, it becomes a societal problem. We become susceptible to political leaders who push our deeply ingrained cultural "buttons" to "divide and conquer."

We need an additional identity.

"I am a citizen."

PATRIOTISM

Patriotism is the quality of love for our country and devotion to it. It is a high-level, abstract concept that requires us to hold a deeply formed image of our country and be loyal to it.

In this book, we focus on followers and leaders of large political entities, most often nations. The leaders of those polities are not usually directly accessible to us. How does our regard for and loyalty to the more accessible leaders in our daily lives—those in our families, workplaces, religious affiliations, and so forth—translate into our relationship with the entire nation?

The root of *patriotism* is *patriarchy*. For the survival of a small clan (which is really an extended family), loyalty to the patriarchy (or occasionally the matriarchy) was essential. When the unit of social organization became more complex in the form of city-states, alliances of city-states, and eventually nation-states, loyalty had to be transferred beyond the existing gene pool to an artificial construct known as a *nation*.

This is generally achieved through the use of symbols and narratives to create a sense of belonging. This is a pro-survival approach to the well-being of larger groups. It also contains risks, as we see throughout history. The narratives of nations become sanitized and hide the shadow side of the nation's formation, consolidation, expansion, and operation. The symbols become fetishes with a near-religious value rather than symbols of inclusion and the rights and duties of citizenship.

There are at least two types of patriotism: *blind patriotism*, in which we never question our country's narrative or policies, and *constructive patriotism*, in which we continually work to make our country even more deserving of our love and support.[5]

As citizens in what we hope to be and remain liberal democracies, we are free to think, formulate, and communicate our beliefs. In this context, patriotism is a choice. As engaged citizens, we work to make the object of that choice—our nation—worthy of our dedication to it. At times, this will require challenging the narrative to make it more truthful and inclusive. At times, we may feel called to withdraw our support for its symbols until the culture and policies behind them better reflect their stated values.

Even if we tend to blind patriotism—to forgive our country its sins and value and honor its many virtues—we must bear this in mind:

Our patriotism is to our nation, not to its leaders.

Political leaders can earn our support as their followers. They can earn our gratitude, even our love, but it is only our country that deserves our patriotic loyalty. Our political leaders, at their best, are the stewards of our nation, entrusted with its care. In contrast, a prototyrant seeks to convince us that they are the only one who can preserve the nation.

A prototyrant will go so far as to claim they are *the nation.*

This claim is one of the strongest warning signs that the leader is on a tyrannical trajectory. When we hear this claim, it is time to go on full alert if we are true patriots.

"SAVIORS" AND VIOLENCE

Would-be saviors, counter to their claims of heralding a better life, often initiate violence to solve problems facing the populace, such as immigration, racial tension, and wealth disparities. They present themselves as a vengeful, sword-wielding messiah. Calls to violence provide an illusion of agency in the lives of citizens who view themselves as disregarded—a seductive illusion that must be recognized.

Who does the implicit or explicit call to violence serve? It rarely, if ever, serves followers who are being incited to commit violence, though perversely, it can seem they are being empowered, as the leader purports to be fighting on their behalf. Helping these followers question who the violence serves is a priority for religious leaders, family members, cultural heroes—all those who have a chance to affect the thinking of these followers.

As followers, we ourselves must be equipped to ask this question of the leader: "You are calling for action against this group or that group, but realistically, what are you proposing to do for us?" We need to require answers that are not bullet points based on the most recent poll but answers with enough flesh on them for us to judge their seriousness and likelihood of success.

A leader who paints the world as darker and the future more apocalyptic than it is has an agenda. The agenda is to set them up as the ones to save the world from this fate. There is always an element of truth in the autocrat's dark vision; that is what hooks us. Our job is to place this in perspective and evaluate the larger picture more clearly—does the vision hold more light than dark? Or is it designed to terrify us into the arms of the self-proclaimed savior?

Yes, there can be the right leader for the right moment in history. In a democracy, candidates for office need to convince the electorate they are better qualified than their rivals to meet the challenges of the moment, so the process creates a necessity for self-promotion. However, their emphasis is on what is needed in the situation, not their superiority.

When you hear the *would-be tyrant sell themselves as the one-and-only savior, t*he best response is deep caution. They are unlikely to be the leader that is needed and, indeed, may be its opposite.

CHAPTER 5

THE POPULACE CIRCLE

The Crowd and the Individual

.

"Since the beginning, it was just the same.
The only difference? The crowds are bigger now."
—ELVIS PRESLEY

POPULISTS

The rise of populists in a democracy is not a flaw in the system. It is a self-correcting mechanism.

Oxford Languages' Google English dictionary defines a *populist* this way:

a person, especially a politician, who strives to appeal to ordinary people who feel that their concerns are disregarded by established elite groups. "He ran as a populist on an anti-corruption platform."

The interests of the economic and political elite often clash with those of the average person. It is nearly inevitable in a democracy that the power of the vote, which lies in the hands of the populace, will be in tension with the power of the economic elite to influence and sway the election and the resulting policies. When these forces are perceived as too opposed, a populist political leader will arise to express the unmet needs of their followers seeking a champion.

If this is a self-correcting mechanism, then it needn't be feared. Or should it?

As we are concerned with the power of the followers, let's look at this. If the populist is only championing the needs of the populace to be better represented in the democratic process and the economic policies it produces, we could rest easy at night. But often, that is not the case.

All people and cultures have what is sometimes called a *dark side* or *shadow*. We needn't go down the path of psychological or spiritual reasons for this, but we should observe and acknowledge the prevalence of this phenomenon. The shadow manifests differently in each culture, depending on its history. It almost always involves persecuting ethnic groups who are perceived as inferior or as a danger to the values and primacy of the dominant group. These become the scapegoat for the real problems the governing system adequately fails to address. And there is the danger.

Rather than deal with the actual and often complex sources of an imbalance in society, the populist with autocratic tendencies will take the easy route of inflaming popular passions against both the elite and these "outsiders" and will target voices who call their toxic strategy into question. With adroit manipulation, they transfix their followers into thinking these oversimplifications are the actual causes of their discontent and that they are the champions willing to smash existing norms to set things right.

How will you, as a potential follower of this populist leader, determine if they are a "good guy" to follow or a dangerous autocrat? Both of these populist types are skilled at firing up the crowd, getting the crowd to believe in them, and suspending or diminishing rational thinking in favor of hope for a champion to right what is wrong with the system. How do we sort out the light and prosocial vision from the dark and dangerous?

And you thought democracy was easy!

BEING SWEPT UP IN MASS RALLIES

In what setting is the populace most likely to be seduced into a populist's worldview?

While telecommunications of every sort bring us into a political leader's "fold," perhaps the most powerful way of binding us to them is the political rally. It is quite remarkable that in this day of virtual communication, tens of thousands of people will line up for hours to hear their favored political candidate address the crowd.

What is going on here?

As sports fans well know, it is seductive to be part of a group of tens of thousands of people chanting the same thing at the same time. It produces a visceral sense of belonging, an adrenaline rush, a high!

In political life, the rally creates close identification with the charismatic leader and the movement they personify. This may be the closest many of us physically get to our most powerful and inspiring political leaders.

While being part of thousands of supporters chanting for a leader is thrilling, political followers should be leery of these dynamics—they drown out rational thinking. We are pulled into a visceral collective response to the leader's incantations. The result may be finding ourselves in an energized state, ready for action. But is this diminishment of our rational reasoning what is needed from the citizenry? Is this the way to choose a governing leader with the power of life and death?

Saying this can create confusion, as populist politicians who do not have tyrannical ambitions use similar techniques for stirring crowd engagement in their calls to action. They need us to bring our energy and heightened commitment to large movements for social betterment or to sweep them into power. We need ways of distinguishing between different types of leaders who use similar tool kits.

When I was a boy, my father used to take me to night games at our home team's baseball stadium. The bright lights on the green outfield created a magical setting as I watched and scored the game play-by-play.

One night, in the seventh-inning stretch, Marilyn Monroe was driven around the field in a body-tight, sequined dress on the hood of an Eldorado convertible Cadillac. I was mesmerized.

Another night, my father took me to an outdoor place I didn't recognize. It was an expansive parking lot in front of a large neighborhood church. There was a speaker's platform at the top of the steps. Diamond-bright lights lit up the platform, like those at the baseball stadium.

My father never talked about politics, but something drew him to this event with thousands of people packed into the space.

The speaker bounded onto the platform. Being shorter than the adults, I couldn't see very well. My father lifted me.

On the platform was a handsome man with a shock of reddish-brown hair and a mile-wide smile of white teeth that reflected the bright lights. I cannot remember what he said, but I will never forget this mesmerizing moment, which rivaled seeing Marilyn Monroe.

Months later, the brilliantly lit speaker, John F. Kennedy, was elected president.

DIFFERENTIATING THE CHARISMATIC REFORMER AND THE PROTOTYRANT

Gifted politicians are often gifted orators. If the charismatic reformer and the prototyrant use similar communication strategies, how do we, as followers, discern the character behind the individuals?

We need to go beyond the soaring rhetoric and power of the call-and-response chant and assess the social value of the content. It is a world of difference to get the crowd chanting,

"Go back to where you came from!" than to create a unifying chorus of "We are all united!"

Once chanting starts, it can take on a life of its own. If you see a video of what you were chanting along with the crowd, there may come a moment when you are dismayed at the hatefulness in the words.

Pay attention to the content of what is being chanted, and make a conscious choice if you want to be associated with that message.

Is the content social or antisocial? Does it support our best cultural values and institutions or undermine them?

Political adversaries may have diametrically opposed views of what policies are in the interest of the country. That is the tension that politics exists to negotiate. But politics only works when there is a shared sense of core values. The reformer is building on our shared values. The prototyrant is tearing them down. They use their firebrand rhetoric to create a frenzy for laying the stepping stones to their inflated sense of destiny.

Emerging tyrants know they must program the populace to respond to their presence. Whether this is with a Nazi salute or a chant of "death to our enemies," the populace is being trained physically, emotionally, and psychologically for resonance with the tyrant and unquestioning faith in them. Ultimately, for obedience.

As citizens, we need to be alert when a loyalty test is implicitly or explicitly imposed by requiring a chant, a salute, a code word.

1936 photo in which a man, thought to be August Landmesser, is conspicuously not giving the Nazi salute

There is a time to stop chanting or cheering.

There is a time to fold our arms across our chest and signify our disapproval of a specific message and perhaps of the leader delivering it.

The window for doing this is before the prototyrant achieves the power that makes it personally dangerous to take even a simple stance like this.

DON'T CREATE A MESSIAH

The cheering and adulation at a sports match is a time-bound event. When the game is over, everyone—contestants, fans, referees—goes home and gets on with their lives.

At a political rally, the candidate for high office doesn't want to go home. They want us to elevate them to the house where the ruler resides and keep them there as long as possible. If the seeker of public office and the power it holds is successful, they become part of our lives for years to come. We can't switch off the "game" when the rally is over. The laws, rules, regulations, executive actions, taxes, declarations of emergency, and trade or foreign policy maneuvers all just keep coming.

Crowd adulation at sporting events energizes athletes. Home team advantage is well-known and valued. In the political world, the consequences are more enduring. Crowd adulation can make the leader feel as though they were called by destiny to lead their people. This self-belief in their destiny is not inherently problematic. It becomes so when they add a layer to the belief that they alone are destined to save their people.

Their followers may come to believe this, too. In a world in which we are vulnerable and lack the power to control our destiny, there is an understandable longing for a champion, even a savior. When this occurs, the cheering followers are not just contributing to a leader's victory. They are reinforcing what we might call *a messiah complex*, which already has a foothold in the leader.

Messiah comes from a Hebrew word meaning *the anointed*. Followers are anointing the leader. This is dangerous, as messiahs are sent to rule the world and can do no wrong. In the political messiah's mind, whatever they do is right, no matter how many may suffer. History is full of would-be messiahs on the so-called political left and right, on the secular and theocratic ends of the spectrum. Among the marquee names who fashioned themselves as the indispensable saviors of their country and became its tyrannical rulers, we can include Napolean Bonaparte, Benito Mussolini, Adolph Hitler, Fidel Castro, and Ayatollah Ruhollah Khomeini.

If a political leader is allowed to assume a messianic identity, they will become impermeable to corrective feedback. After all, they are the messiah, the chosen one. Who are we to question them? Whatever their flaws, their tendencies, their autocratic instincts, all of these will become exaggerated.

This dangerous tendency can be reinforced at rallies right before our eyes. The leader may slip hateful rhetoric into the chant-and-response pattern. The crowd no longer pays attention to the sense of any specific statement. They repeat the hateful rhetoric as one great beast roaring at the world. They have been mesmerized by the spell the leader is casting.

What is worse, the leader has been mesmerized and validated by their followers. They know they are the beloved leader! While sowing the seeds of dissension, they become evermore certain they are doing the right thing.

Yes, there are discreet points where robustly vocalizing enthusiasm for a specific policy idea is appropriate and healthy. Let out a roar of approval. This is different from mindlessly cheering for everything the populist leader is saying, claiming, and promising, on and on and on. Even if you love the candidate, resist the mindless chant of the crowd. Be the model for responsible following. Fold your arms across your chest. Give others the courage to do the same.

Followers create leaders. Create a leader, not a messiah.

CROWDS AND THEIR ANTIDOTE

A number of scholars examine the almost mystical effect crowds have in transforming individual behavior into a collective trance, which can be transporting but also dispose the collective to violence.

Elias Canetti, in his classic work on crowds, observed that a change occurs in a crowd where people lose their sense of individuality and crave feeling part of a powerful and willful mass event. In this altered state, the capacity for rational, ethical thinking and compassion for others is greatly reduced.[1]

If we are at a mass rally and experience a degree of sympathy for the target of the authoritarian ire—usually a member of a minority—while those around do not, it is a sign we are on the periphery of an evolving tyrannical culture. This is equivalent to being on the rim of a black hole. If we cross the event horizon, there is no return. It is a choice point: Retain the human quality of sympathy for the other or quash this to comply with the prototyrant's exhortations.

Healthy followership requires a capacity and willingness to examine ideas, look at them within the context of one's own experience, and accept or refute them. This capacity is antipathetic to the state that forms in a crowd in which individual examination virtually ceases to exist. Can we practice individual thinking while being part of a crowd, like world-class figure skaters, who focus on their performance, not the roaring fans? We do not have years of training like professional athletes. A corrective may be forming small dialogue groups during breaks in the speeches or after the event to rebalance ourselves—but not a small group that is an echo chamber. What is needed?

THE SMALL GROUP AND DIALOGUE

It is understood that messages must be focused and distilled in mass rallies. This is not the time and place for the nuanced dialogue of small groups, which can precede or follow the collective event.

Large political rallies are necessary to project follower-ship power, straddling the continuum between speech and action. Used well, they contribute to checking the progression toward tyrannical behavior or forwarding the values of leaders who stand as constructive alternatives to the would-be tyrant.

Even as the world makes greater use of communications technology, there is a trend for using that technology to initiate, coordinate, protect, and amplify the message of the physical crowd. That technology can also be used to form thousands of small groups to further dialogue about the events. These can deepen our understanding and commitment to lifting positive leadership and interrupting the rise of those who would abuse the power entrusted to them.

The 1960s were a time of mass protest movements on university campuses. These took the form of rallies, marches, sit-ins, boycotts, and other tactics. One that is not often cited is the "teach-in." As formal classes were disrupted, demonstrators self-organized into smaller groups in which there was an opportunity for detailed analyses of the issues and sufficient dialogue to deepen the understanding of those participating.

You will readily see how this counterbalances the hours-long speeches and harangues of autocrats vying for or attempting to consolidate political power. The curious mind, the questioning mind, and the empathetic mind all become engaged in determining the needs and strategies for the way forward. Poll-driven manipulation by a charismatic demagogue meets its match in the distributed information, diverse perspectives, and power of decentralized groups. Use of these small communication pods can keep the large outer circle of political followers thinking agilely and prepared to withstand attempts to manipulate and control them. This is the first layer of followership defense from the wiles of prototyrannical leaders.

NOT JUST ANY SMALL GROUP

The physicality of the mass crowd is inhospitable to conversation and, thus, to rational reflection on what is being felt, heard, and experienced. However, the same can be true of the small group if it is used as a tool of indoctrination instead of genuine dialogue.

Conversations as an antidote to prototyrannical indoctrination require small group participants to listen to each other and be interested in understanding others' experiences, not debating or converting them.

It can start with broad questions like these:

What did you hear? What response did that evoke in you?

Small group reflections balance large crowd events.

How does what was said compare to your own experience and views?

If nothing else, invitations like these bring the thinking mind back "online," creating distinctions between rhetoric and reality. If we go to a movie theater, we will talk about the movie with friends over dinner: what we liked, what we didn't get, what troubled us. Surely, doing so after a political gathering is at least as useful for making sense of the experience.

The obvious challenge to the value of this exercise is avoiding replicating the information bubble of the larger group. This is easier said than done. We hang out with others who are like-minded. However, in the safety and thoughtfulness that a small group permits, perhaps we will find significant differences even among our allies.

We can also get more daring. In all political systems, those at opposite ends of the spectrum are given names.

Sometimes, they are formal (Labour vs. Conservative), sometimes they are geographical (North vs. South), or as simple as colors (red vs. blue or green). Use imagination and technology to extend invitations across ideological divides. It takes someone to initiate that conversation, to explain its purpose and the ground rules for listening to each other. Why not let this "someone" be you?

I have met with several groups that used a "talking stick" to deepen listening among group members. Here is a synthesis of how this might look.

Janette Speaks-With-Lions grew up in a traditional tribal family. They had their problems, maybe more than their share.

One thing they did well was circle meetings. She loved the talking stick, decorated with a deep indigo dye, that was passed around the circle. Whoever held it spoke. Others listened.

Janette learned much in these circles. Even the quiet ones had interesting things to say. The elders were respected. The young were heard.

She was stunned at how different this was from the virtual communications outside her community. In truth, those were not conversations: They were shouting matches with shaming splattered on everyone like the mud thrown up by tricked-out motorcycles on the main drag.

She learned little, so she left those virtual sites and began her own group elsewhere. The first thing she did was create a meme—an indigo-feathered talking stick—and made it available to others.

THE ROLE OF OUR PEERS

At all levels of followership, we must be conscious of how we form our beliefs. Many of us have learned the importance of staying alert when reading electronic posts to determine which are likely accurate and which are suspect.

However, there is another source of information that requires awareness: our peers.

The constructivist theory of learning posits that starting from an early age, much of our learning comes from our peers. Like all matters of human interaction, this has potential upsides and downsides.

When we learn from our peers, we usually see them as friends or role models, informed or experienced in areas we are not. Our understandable bias is to trust them until proven otherwise. If our peer believes an individual or group is untrustworthy, we are prone to incorporate their belief into our view of the world without sufficiently inspecting it or testing it against other perspectives.

In the political realm, one or more of our peers may voice strong support for a political leader, though that leader is showing early authoritarian signs. The passion of our peer's belief can be persuasive, or it may contain a tinge of shaming and bullying. They may have already influenced several other mutual friends to share their viewpoint. Socially, the easiest course of action would be to fall in line with our peers' thinking. But how quickly we would become a colluder!

We all have one or two friends or colleagues who are highly opinionated. They're often smart as well. It would be useful to question our opinionated peer about their views to determine whether they are based on good data and reasoning or if those views are no more than overly confident assertions, colloquially and correctly referred to as "hot air." If we can do this with an attitude of nonjudgmental interest, we may open space for our peer to reexamine their stance. In any case, by questioning, we are interrupting indiscriminate social contagion, which is no small thing.

In the twentieth century, we witnessed multiple examples of destructive social contagion, events such as the Hutu and Tutsi mutual killings in the hundreds of thousands with machetes and clubs in 1994 in Rwanda. We have witnessed it in the mass extermination of Jews in Europe in the first half of the twentieth century and Chairman Mao's Cultural Revolution in the latter half of the century, in which millions of young Chinese berated, beat, and buried their elders and better-off fellow citizens.

While it is easy to express dismay at these historical examples, it is important to recognize that social contagion, like viral or bacterial pandemics, continues to occur throughout the world. You and I are potential carriers of this contagion. We are, therefore, responsible for inoculating ourselves from this prospect. With self-awareness and social courage, rather than contagion spreading, we can be a firebreak and exert positive peer influence.

There is a moment of choice when we can go along with incendiary language or call it out and stand up for principle. We can do this without refuting the leader but rather calling for more constructive behavior while we are in the window for doing so. If the leader does not step through that window with us, then we need to consider our alternatives thoughtfully. This is the essence of ethical followership.

I was at a conference on followership as the path to leadership at the US Naval Academy. I had been a panelist on followership and ethics.

The keynote speech that evening was being given in the basketball stadium by a former vice president of the United States. The stadium was full. The vice presidency is a quintessential follower role. I was prepared to be interested in the speaker's remarks about the conference theme. He made none. Instead, he used the entire speech to justify what is now widely considered to be a disastrous foreign policy of which he had been a key architect.

At the conclusion of his speech, the entire stadium rose in robust applause. I was stunned that the applause was anything more than polite. I did not rise from my seat or applaud; neither did the individual next to me, who had also been a presenter in the program. I am not sure I would have been able to remain seated without the implicit support of a peer who resisted the roar of the crowd. Perhaps he would not either if I had stood.

CROWDS THAT DO POSITIVE THINGS

I recently saw a photograph of the famous Woodstock Music Festival in 1969 that attracted an estimated 400,000 concertgoers. Young people were sitting on the hillside as far as the eye could see. The caption marveled at how little police crowd control was needed as people self-organized to help each other through the logistics of a three-day encampment with few supporting services.

This was emblematic of the enormous crowds that, at times, materialize for a religious event or in support of protecting or changing a government whose legitimacy is in question. Many positive contemporary examples exist.

In 1989, two decades after Woodstock, one such event was the Baltic Chain of two million people that stretched six hundred kilometers through the capitals of Estonia, Latvia, and Lithuania in support of independence from the occupation of the Soviet Union. Seven months later, Lithuania became the first Soviet republic to declare independence.

Crowds themselves are not a problem when they maintain their sense of human connection and mutual care. The individuals who compose the crowd, to a degree, transcend their identity and assume that of the crowd. But they do not relinquish their humanity and responsibility for maintaining this in their speech and acts.

Organize

Crowds can form spontaneously in response to a perceived outrage. They also form on cue in well-planned

Map data ©2024 by Google

demonstrations for or against policies, political rallies, and symbolic gatherings. But paradoxically, the real power of the crowd is when it disperses and organizes itself into meaningful action groups connected by strong communication networks.

Large numbers of well-organized people who can be mobilized to withstand encroaching or established oppression are the counterweight to the machinery erected around the emerging or entrenched political tyrant. Organizing is itself an exercise in leadership and followership. When done on a populace-wide level, it provides the body politic with alternative systems to those of an oppressive regime.

The story of strongman rule in Sudan under former dictator Omar al-Bashir is an all-too-familiar story of coming to power in a coup d'état, serving under various titles for twenty years, and being removed by another coup two decades later.

What interests us here is that leading up to his ouster, the Sudanese organized themselves into thousands of neighborhood "resistance committees" nationwide. These were originally the vehicles for protesting the tyrannical use of power and the harm brought by corruption, repression, and wars of aggression.

Many of these committees went on to provide support for elections and public welfare, where the government had left a vacuum in meeting these needs. Regarding these committees, the *Economist* notes, "The committees offer a glimpse of how ordinary people were able to come together to fight for freedom."[2]

These communal acts are no panacea. At this writing, South Sudan continues to be racked by corruption and internal conflict. But neither are they negligible from a humanitarian or a psychological perspective. In addition to providing communal self-sufficiency, perhaps as important is how they are an antidote to the sense of helplessness individuals feel about the suffocating power of a tyrannical state. In this sense, they are mobilizers of the latent power of the populace to lift itself up and insulate itself from run-amok rulers.

REFLECTIONS ON THE POWER OF THE POPULACE

A populist leader may genuinely work in the nation's interests, seeking to raise the wealth of the country and create conditions in which those who contribute to that wealth receive their fair share. They earn their followers.

It is when the populist with autocratic tendencies begins morphing into a tyrant that the risks outweigh the benefits. The "trick" is to notice when the leader moves to accrue greater power to themselves. That is when we enter the "window" in which there is still an opportunity to interrupt this progression. The window only stays open for so long. If we fail to act decisively at that time, the leader's autocratic impulses move to consolidate their power. Once power is consolidated, we lose the political space in which to make a difference.

We are one of many. A "nobody." How do we stand up against both the leader and the crowd? We have the power to stop applauding and raise cautionary notes that can get those around us to reconsider their support as well. We may decide to move into an activist role to organize resistance to the changes that offend our values and endanger our institutions.

This willingness to review our thinking and increasing dependence on a self-proclaimed savior begins the change process. Externally, it manifests in the counterrally, in the vote, and other political actions. It denies the prototyrant victory, perhaps in a crucial referendum to weaken constitutional checks on their power, perhaps in elevating their cronies to positions of power.

If this is done in time and with sufficient resolve, we may be able to save the leader from their own worst impulses. The nation wins. So do we. Remember that we are always dealing with the leader, the followers, and the context. In each context, there will be different levers that can be pulled, various mechanisms for applying braking pressure to what threatens to become a runaway train,

If the situation becomes more dire, we will need the cooperation of other circles of followers to create a transition of power. We will examine each of these circles and the potential for coordinated action between them.

The only thing more powerful than a leader is their followers.

POPULACE	SUMMARY
Available Information	Autocrat pronouncements, popular media
Incentives to Follow	Enhanced social identity and material promises
Vulnerability	Susceptible to charisma/wish for a savior
Risks	Social and economic costs of dissent
Communication Channels	Mass rallies and social media
Courage Needed	Standing apart from the crowd
Power to Influence	Collective—mass shows of support or disaffection

CHAPTER 6

The Activist Circle

The Threat and Responsibility

.

"My grandmother used to say, 'In the Bronx, you don't ask
one person to do what is right. You ask the whole block.'"
—US television series *Law & Order*

WHAT IS AN ACTIVIST?

Circle 5 Populace
Circle 4 Activists
Circle 3 Bureaucrats
Circle 2 Elites
Circle 1 Confidants

LEADER

Inner Circle
Near Inner Circle
Middle Circle
Near Outer Circle
Outer Circle

Activists are the linchpin between significant segments of the populace and the aspirational or sitting political leader. While the populace goes about its business of daily living, the activist makes political change their business.

There are always activists organizing people and resources in support of a charismatic political leader and opposition to them. Both are working with similar tool kits to persuade the populace for or against the leader who is capturing their attention. They are striving to bring the power of the populace to acclaim or depose the leader, to ram through or block consequential policies.

Activism is not primarily a rational act. It is not necessarily irrational, but it is driven by passion: a passion for or against an ideal, a justice or injustice, a savior of a way of life, or a grave threat to it. Without this passion, activists would not expend the energy and time stolen from ordinary acts of life and transfer them to the crusade.

Activists are a force to change the world; whether that change is beneficial or dystopic will be a function of the leader they have chosen as their standard-bearer. Activists are force multipliers. In their vigorous support of the leader, they are worth a thousand members of the populace; in their energetic opposition to the leader, they are as threatening as a mob at the palace gates.

If they stand out in their success as supportive activists, they will be promoted within the leader's organization. If they are perceived as threats to an autocrat's designs on power, they will be targeted to be neutralized. Activists are individuals who disregard the caution that the nail that sticks up is the first to be hammered down. By their creative actions, they are leaders; by their advocacy, they are followers, supportive or disapproving of the leader's agenda and style.

The activist is not content with watching history being made; they may be bit-players, but they are players. As players, they share accountability for the movement's success or failure, the leader at its head, and the consequences of the forces they unleash.

In my democracy-building work in West Africa, I saw the tensions between the traditional Big Man way of doing things and emerging new ways. This is the type of scenario that might occur, showing the difficulty of this transformation.

Ndaleh was a good girl. She learned the crafts she would need to know at the feet of her mother and her gran. She was a bright girl. She was sent to school, where her curiosity about the world was encouraged. She always knew that men held positions of power, but here, she began to see another kind of power—women's power.

When Estelle Oloare challenged the power structure by naming herself a candidate for public office, Ndaleh began supporting her campaign. She was good at convincing other women to support her candidate. When Oloare upset the male power structure, Ndaleh was exhilarated.

Once in office, Oloare began emulating the behaviors of the men; she made too many side deals with cronies. Ndaleh was disappointed. In the next campaign, she could

continued

not bring herself to support Oloare. She stood on an old wooden box to explain why to the people who would listen. Her friend Asa videoed her speech and posted it.

The next day, her supervisor told Ndaleh she was no longer employed. Others said they were not interested in hiring her. She felt the sting of being on the bad side of an officeholder. Now, she needed to get on with her life. Perhaps one day, she would be the candidate.

Activists bear extra responsibility for awareness of the values they are empowering, and for discerning the truth or falsity of the claims the leader is making that they are trying to sell to the populace.

DO NOT BE IN AWE OF POLITICAL LEADERS

Activists are the converter and amplifier that takes the charismatic leader's message and connects it with the lives of the populace. If they support the leader, they propel their ascendence; if they oppose the leader, they warn the populace of their potential excesses. Let's start with the proponents of the leader.

Putting our heart into a cause is a life-changing move. We are energized with a sense of purpose that we may not have previously experienced. Often, when we do this, there is a leader who represents that cause. Our love for the cause spills into adulation for the leader who personifies it. When the leader and the cause become indivisible in our mind, the glow of the cause infuses and can significantly distort our perception of the leader.

I shrank in horror to read the writing of David Ben-Gurion, the democratically elected first prime minister of Israel, on his earlier devotion to Vladimir Lenin, who became the supreme leader of the newly formed Soviet Union. Lenin also became the model for his brutal successor, Josef Stalin. Listen to Ben-Gurion's alarming infatuation with Lenin and the characteristics of a tyrant:

> **A man who disdains all obstacles, faithful to his goal, who knows no concessions or discounts, the extreme of extremes, who knows how to crawl on his belly in the utter depths in order to reach his goal; a man of iron will who does not spare human life and the blood of innocent children for the sake of revolution. . . . the naked reality, the cruel truth, and the reality of power relations will be before his sharp and clear eyes . . . the single goal, burning with red flame—the goal of the great revolution.**[1]

Imagine Ben-Gurion, decades later, having witnessed the immense oppression of the Jewish people by the Soviet regime. Why could he not see the writing on the wall when supporting the fierce ruthlessness of a tyrant? Yet, he is not alone. History is strewn with examples of those giving decades of service to a revolutionary leader only to find their revolution betrayed by that leader and themselves exiled or imprisoned.

At this juncture in history, that is the fate of many of the Sandinistas in Nicaragua who overthrew a brutal tyrant in the 1970s only to now live under another *democratically elected* president who has himself become a tyrant, their former revolutionary leader, Daniel Ortega. As of this writing, Ortega has held the presidency for seventeen years, ruthlessly quashing all democratic attempts to unseat him.

Will they come for me? What will it be like to be jailed by the same people I fought alongside to topple the 45-year Somoza dictatorship in Nicaragua, my country? . . . Now, the man once chosen to represent our hope for change, Daniel Ortega, has become another tyrant . . . many of us wanted to modernize the Sandinista movement. Mr. Ortega would have none of it. He viewed our attempts to democratize the party as a threat to his control . . . Nicaraguans now find ourselves with no recourse, no law, no police to protect us . . . I am an outspoken critic of Mr. Ortega. I tweet, I give interviews. Under Mr. Somoza, I was tried for treason. I had to go into exile. Will I now face jail or exile again?

Who will they come for next?

—GIOCONDA BELLI, Nicaraguan poet and novelist[2]

When we give our heart and soul to a cause, we will have fewer regrets if we also use our brains and keep an engaging leader separated in our minds from the cherished cause. We reserve our critical thinking faculties not to conflate the emerging tyrannical profile with the cherished cause.

"If you hold up a leader as a paragon of virtue, you may aid in consolidating their power, which can have all kinds of unintended consequences."
—ELIZABETH SAUNDERS,
George Washington University political scientist

Only by keeping this separation clear will activists provide accountable leadership to those they are encouraging to follow. Creeds are not always easy to live up to, but they identify what we hope to honor by our actions. Here is a possible creed for activist followership:

I love this cause.

I am committed to this cause.

I believe this leader can propel this cause forward.

But they are not the cause.

Like each of us, they will serve the cause imperfectly.

I will not expect perfection.

Neither will I allow myself to be in awe of them.

The ends do not justify brutality.

If they misuse the support we give them, I will speak up.

I owe this to the cause I cherish and people I enlist in its support.

I will not always prevail but will always remain principled.

THE ACTIVIST AS ETHICAL FOLLOWER AND LEADER

The political activist is a quintessential example of vigorous leadership and followership embodied in the same individual.

Unless they themselves are seeking political office, activists are in support of a party or candidate who is seeking public office or an incumbent officeholder. From that perspective, they are followers of the political leader.

At the same time, these individuals are often particularly creative and innovative in their activism. In this sense, they are leaders. They are a primary example of how followership is not a passive or weak role but rather one that can be performed with ingenuity, commitment, energy, and, yes, leadership!

As leaders, they bring along the community to support issues they are championing and the political candidates embracing those issues. They create followers.

As strong, accountable followers, they are committed to making the leader successful. This commitment carries with it a responsibility to be aware of, and at times constructively critical, of the political leader. The ethical follower holds the leader accountable for being true to their expressed values through language and actions.

The ethical dimensions of their actions take on a particularly pronounced role because their actions are not simply choices that they make for themselves. They are simultaneously persuading others to act alongside them.

If activists begin to harbor doubts about the leader's ethics or autocratic tendencies but continue to persuade others to support the leader, they betray both themselves and those they seek to influence. They have a dual duty—to their conscience and the people they are influencing—to pause and examine the source of their concerns. If they find substance in their concerns, they must pivot and aim their energy back toward the political leader, effectively conveying their concerns. If the leadership is open to hearing and considering their validity and finding better ways of pursuing their agenda, the political leader deserves their continued support.

If their concerns are met with deaf ears and harsh criticism, this validates the activist's concerns. It is at the early stage of the political leader seeking power that the activist can make a difference in the trajectory of the use of power.

Ethical action is timely action. It is the window that needs to be recognized and utilized while the political situation is still malleable. It is the pivot point of following and leading in a political relationship.

THE CULTURE YOU COCREATE
WITH THE LEADER

In a democratic system, all are free to support the political leader or candidate of their choice. None have a crystal ball to foretell how a candidate will perform once elected or how they will evolve in office. Who you choose to support as an activist may be diametrically opposed to my choice, and both still have legitimacy.

Given the reality of political diversity in a genuinely democratic culture, who we support is equally important to *how* we provide that support.

Activists always seek to boost their candidate's chances of success. That is only natural but is not itself an ethical standard. If the means generate high levels of distrust that tear apart the polity, it fails an ethical standard for democratic self-governance. How is this so?

The ethical activist envisions an alternative future that improves lives rather than painting a dystopic picture of what life would be under the alternative candidate. Mind you, this goes against the counsel of political operatives who urge their candidate to portray their opponent in the most frightening terms possible.

When both sides rely on creating fear of apocalyptic futures under the adversary, the populace is thrown into high anxiety and trauma. Look around you now. Is this the environment in which both sides are living? Fear for the very existence of the state if the other side is victorious?

In extreme moments of history, sadly, this may be true. However, we need to be alert that our culture may be creating an atmosphere of hyperanxiety regardless of who the competing candidates or parties are. This caution does not preclude warning of authoritarian trends but does not make doing so the primary focus.

The appropriate mindset that supports positive activism is that of competitors in a contest of compelling vision and demonstrated skill, not of gladiators in mortal combat.

The activist may need to discern among the various signals coming from the leader and choose which to amplify. If they amplify messages that generate fear and hate, and likely voters respond receptively to these, the office seeker with autocratic tendencies will take notice. They will be encouraged to deliver more of this "red meat" to the crowd. The slippery slope will become increasingly treacherous, with few footholds to stop the descent into a hopelessly antagonistic citizenry.

If, instead, the activist identifies and reinforces the prosocial platform embedded in the candidacy, the leader may observe the effectiveness of this approach and turn to healthier paths to political power. If the candidate successfully enters office, they will have become accustomed to those around them supporting this prosocial path. Ideally, they will continue to cocreate it, if only out of self-interest in retaining popular support.

Once again, this is a case of the follower subtly leading.

At the same time, the activist must stay alert. If the candidate or officeholder continues to spew deep division and toxic scenarios, it is time to reconsider their activism on behalf of this leader. If the fires of activism continue to burn within them, it may be time to turn their organizing skills to support a more prosocial leader, one with compatible political ideology unpolluted by metastasizing authoritarian behavior.

The activist is creating and enabling the culture in which they, too, will need to live. Victory at all costs may be a price too high to pay.

Lee Atwater, a rock and roll band guitarist, became a political activist in South Carolina in the 1970s. His activism on behalf of Republican members of Congress became a path to consulting on the premier elections of his time—Ronald Reagan and George H. W. Bush—despite his young thirty-something years of age. This was a case of activism being rewarded and the activist being drawn into the elite circle of followers, even the inner circle of confidants.

Though boyish in appearance, Atwater practiced cutthroat politics. He had a keen sense for issues that would divide the electorate and stampede them to his party and candidates. He set the tone for distorting facts and ruthlessly exploiting cultural fracture lines, particularly about race. Using Atwater as the role model of his age, politics became a blood sport.

In March 1990, Atwater fainted publicly. Tests revealed an aggressive brain tumor. A year later, at the age of forty, he was dead.

In the months remaining to him, Atwater tried making amends with political opponents he had brutally misrepresented. He recognized that politics needed a large infusion of heart, not the venom he was injecting.

Some say this deathbed conversion was for show. I am not convinced that is so. I prefer to apply Samuel Johnson's observation to the matter.

"Depend upon it, sir. When a man knows he is to be hanged in a fortnight, it concentrates his mind wonderfully."

ACTIVISTS AS MORAL AGENTS

There are several classic books on the subject of organizing others for social and political change. Undoubtedly, there are equally vibrant treatises in other media where the collective experience of contemporary organizers and activists can be studied.

These classics may be effective road maps for activists. They are not necessarily ethical road maps. In his famous book, *Rules for Radicals,* the political progressive Saul Alinsky acknowledges that for many issues, the relative right-vs.-wrong of competing sides may be close to 50-50, but that a radical activist must ignore this and claim the validity of their case to be near 100, while that of their opponent is near zero.[3]

That may be effective in riling up an audience and enrolling their support, but what effect does it have on the societal framework where governing must take place? If it erodes the societal framework on which communal life depends, it is inherently unethical. Therefore, I argue against these damn-the-truth activist strategies.

Political morality transcends winning at any cost. It contemplates the meta effects of how the fight is pursued and what resentments it will leave in its wake. It searches

TO STOP A TYRANT

for paths that do not sunder the bond that is required to maintain a sense of common purpose. Politics occurs when competing interests are vying over governing philosophies and resources within a common framework. Politics ceases if the framework is broken, and a cold or hot war begins.

Activists, more than most citizens, spend an inordinate amount of time tracking political developments. I suggest that activists on all sides of an issue give a similar level of attention to the ethics of the choices being made by political leaders. Are they preserving the common fabric or sowing seeds of discord in the name of expediency and power? This begins with awareness of how we are absorbing a leader's pronouncements. Do those pronouncements appear helpful or do they need questioning? As activists, if we are not willing to entertain both possibilities, that itself is a sign we are too enthralled by a fallible individual.

Questioning leaders should not require heroism or be viewed as disloyalty. It is an integral part of healthy political followership. That is not to suggest that fractiousness and splintering are desirable. These will often be fomented by an autocratic leader who does not wish any single group powerful enough to challenge them. This is another distinction to which activists must remain alert.

Moral leadership and followership work to identify and preserve the right common ground for the group while pursuing specific goals. Tactics that trammel that common ground deserve vigorous questioning by the activists who create the bond between the leader and the citizenry. It can be viewed as their sacred trust.

VULNERABILITIES OF ACTIVISTS

The vulnerabilities of activists are the vulnerabilities of true believers. If they become certain that what the world needs is this particular leader or what the leader stands for, they are prone to suspend judgment about that leader and block out diverging assessments.

There may also be a structural change to their morality. Anything that will aid the leader's ascension to power is moral; anything that impedes that ascension is immoral. They sincerely believe this.

Years later, some will look back at this stage of their life and wonder how they could have been consumed by the fervent hope for a savior. What are the safeguards if you are the activist and recognize that your ardor for this leader may be creating blind spots?

The safeguards are simple yet crucial. They are to find someone whom you have trusted or admired who does not share your wholehearted belief in this leader and movement. Invite them to share their candid perspectives. Listen respectfully. Don't accept or reject their viewpoint, but do identify the two or three most significant concerns they are voicing.

With those concerns in mind, begin to pay close attention to the leader's behavior. Observe for yourself if these concerns show up in what the leader says or does. If they do, expand the dialogue with your trusted source and repeat the observation process to get a more objective view of the leader. You can then make an informed decision on what to do about your support for the leader.

If the activist is one who is standing *in opposition* to

the emerging tyrant, the phenomena are somewhat different. The very fact that they are resisting the trend that is sweeping the culture places them in a state of questioning. This continued questioning differentiates the morally alert activist from the activist whose morality is suspended or inverted. At the same time, it can blind them to the reasons the emerging tyrant is garnering as much support as they are from the populace.

This blindness can result in a form of arrogance that reduces the capacity to speak to those they wish to alert to the dangers they perceive. The safeguard against this is similar: Find someone who *supports* the political leader whom you perceive is a potential tyrant. Listen carefully to how they arrive at their perspective. This will be hard, as you are passionately convinced of the dangers their political champion represents. Nevertheless, if you are serious about your work as an activist, you will cultivate the empathy and self-management to listen and seek to understand. Only when the other individual feels genuinely heard might they open up to listening to your deep reservations.

"HOW" IS AS IMPORTANT AS "WHAT"

How activists act is at least as important as *what* they are attempting, either in support of or in opposition to the political leader.

If they support the leader because they believe that the individual will bring the country the type of leadership it needs, then they act as their representative on the ground. Does this individual convey inspiration or fear to the populace they are mobilizing? Whatever they are bringing now is what will be ascendant if they prevail. Both the activists and those being influenced by them would do well to bear this in mind.

The thought that the end justifies the means, and the means will become more palatable when the leader gains and consolidates power, is delusory. The means employed now will be the blueprint for the means that are used and accentuated when in power.

If activists are countering the sitting or aspiring political leader, there is a temptation to fight fire with fire, to not bind themselves to ethical constraints that the autocrat has no compunction about violating. This risks signaling to the populace they are trying to win over that neither side is better than the other, so they might as well support the one with the most obvious power. The principled activist must live their principles in the way they counter the prototyrant. This does not require pulling punches; indeed, it is important to punch as hard as the prototyrant but always with the goal of strengthening the institutions that will ultimately constrain the leader.

Visible acts of compassion and competence are potentially more powerful in winning the hearts of the populace than visible acts of violence and terror. It is by tapping the deep prosocial instincts and needs of the populace that the anti-authoritarian activist has a strategic advantage. To maintain this advantage, they must not give the autocrat ammunition to portray them otherwise. Significant discipline is required within their ranks, including checking fellow activists whose actions may undermine the advantage of their public impression as "the good guys."

Protecting the movement's good name also requires vigilance against the "agent provocateur," an agent of the autocrat planted to bring discredit to the movement by their behavior. This is a tactic as old as autocracy. One cannot always identify and neutralize the provocateur before they act and bring negative media scrutiny on the group. Once the agent is identified, using that same media to expose the provocateur must be swift and effective.

The Smithsonian's National Air and Space Museum in Washington, DC, was shut down Saturday after a crowd of protesters showed up to voice their opposition to US drone strikes. The march was organized by an antiwar group called October 11 but was quickly joined by some members of the Occupy Wall Street offshoot Occupy DC.

Ten or so protesters tried to force their way past security and were pepper-sprayed in return. One was Patrick Howley, an editor at the conservative magazine *The American Spectator*, who shoved his way into the museum even after being pepper-sprayed. "As far as anyone knew, I was part of this cause—a cause that I had infiltrated the day before in order to mock and undermine [it] in the pages of *The American Spectator*."[4]

In the passionate struggle to impede or unseat a prototyrant, the temptation of using their unscrupulous methods is best resisted and replaced with nimble, creative, and surprising countermoves that keep the populace hopeful and even entertained by their originality and ultimate decency. These make for very good media content and quickly spread among the populace.

THE ACTIVIST'S CHANGING MEGAPHONE

Every age has its megaphone. In an earlier age it was the town crier until they were replaced by the printing press. In the American Revolution, pamphleteers and broadsides vied to create sympathy for the Crown or for those challenging its unrepresentative premises. In the mid-twentieth century, hidden radio transmitters kept subjected populations informed of developments that rulers attempted to hide from the populace. Posters and slogans on building walls and fences have been "the poor man's megaphone."

In the age when this book is written, what we know as *social media*, disseminated on a vast, globally interconnected array of electronic computers, is used creatively to perpetuate the narratives of would-be tyrants and to counter these by agile activists. If I were qualified to describe the innovative use of the best of these ever-evolving tools—which I am not—they would undoubtedly sound antiquated three years from this writing, perhaps even before publication. The details of the media are ever-changing. Their centrality in the activist's tool kit is not. There are a daunting number of ways in which an increasingly autocratic government can outrightly, indirectly, or clandestinely interfere with the channels of communication. There will always be a cat-and-mouse game of the aspiring tyrant attempting to silence the activist and the activist trying to outwit those massively funded efforts.

The activist becomes an artist, an entertainer, an inventor, and an entrepreneur in the identification and use of the megaphone of their era. The earlier they develop these skills and capabilities within their movement, the better the chance of shaping the message that defines the project of the prototyrant in the hearts of the populace.

In our current age of social media platforms, the activists' energy may need to be directed as much to influence the platforms that carry their messages as the prototyrant's efforts at oppression. If the platforms stay resolute in their access to independent voices, their significant weight may counter the power of the prototyrant's regime, at least long enough for activists to devise new avenues of communication as old ones are denied to them.

If activists are not successful in interrupting the progression to tyranny, whatever platform is established will eventually be blocked or shut down by the regime. Their efforts were not in vain. A meaningful percentage of the populace will have had their minds kept fluid with information and perspectives that counter the prototyrant's indoctrination machine. These hold the potential to defang the emerging tyrant when a future opening presents itself.

After the fall of the Soviet Union, the great dissident and playwright Václev Havel became president of Czechoslovakia. Through a democratic process, Slovakia elected to separate from the Czech Republic. What had been the Parliament building stood empty in Prague.

Although now in a position of governing power, the former dissident's antennae remained presciently alert for the potential of the Russian Federation to attempt a resurrection of its sphere of dictatorial control.

During the Cold War, Radio Free Europe and Radio Liberty (the Russian language service) had been funded by the US Congress. The US-sponsored "radios" had been broadcasting for decades into countries in which the Soviet Union controlled the local media, providing the population with more realistic assessments of events that impacted their countries. The Soviets spent enormous amounts of energy blocking the transmissions, and the people were endlessly inventive in creating ways around those blocks, as is the contemporary case with social media under repressive governments.

With the threat of an expansionist Soviet Union apparently gone, Congress had cut the Radios' funding by two-thirds, which would have meant the end of two-thirds of the sixteen Eastern European languages in which they broadcast. In one of Havel's preemptive acts, he invited Radio Free Europe/Radio Liberty to relocate from its expensive headquarters in Munich, Germany, to the vacant Parliament building in Prague for the symbolic sum of one dollar a year.

The move by Havel enabled RFE/RL to keep offering independent programming in all the major Eastern

continued

European and Central Asian languages until developments demonstrate no further need for this in countries that consolidate their democracy. Recent events show us that this process is still fluid and vulnerable to reversals. Of course, the media platforms have changed with the times and now include streaming services and podcasts.

It is true that Radio Free Europe and Radio Liberty were initially funded by the US Central Intelligence Agency. CIA involvement with the radios ended in the early 1970s when they became publicly funded by the US Congress. Serious advocates of a free press, like Havel, were confident in their independent reporting. I was a consultant in the migration from Munich to Prague and was impressed by the journalistic professionalism of the operation.

STRATEGY, TACTICS, AND POLITICALLY BILINGUAL COMMUNICATION

Individual members of the populace are carried along on the wave of collective fervor for the leader or against that leader's policies and political ascension. Activists work overtime to create that fervor.

The skilled activists are politically bilingual—they translate the leader's messages into the vernacular that is meaningful in the lives of the populace. They translate the populace's needs and messages into policy demands for the bureaucrats and elites who can create programs for transforming the social landscape.

The skilled activist is aware that simple slogans keep popular sentiment energized but real change will take coordinated action between forces within the circles closer to the center of power. To mobilize those forces requires a sophisticated understanding of the interests of the different parties and blocs in these circles. That understanding will need to be woven into campaigns that speak to the most influential of these players and trigger the fewest oppositional forces.

At the center of the calculation is the gravity exerted on the system by the charismatic leader who can disrupt its inertia and catalyze change. It becomes the activists' responsibility to assess if that disruption is likely to lead to the freedoms and social benefits the leader claims. Or is it more likely that the disruption will result in freedoms being lost and funds meant for social benefit being pilfered?

While the populace is earning its living, enjoying their families, and participating in the entertainment earned as productive members of society, the activist is huddling in small groups to develop strategy. This is three- or four-dimensional chess, as there are always other groups simultaneously developing different strategies or counterstrategies.

The successful activist balances political acumen with core principles. If you think this is an easy task, try walking a tightrope over the Grand Canyon—tip a little too far in either direction, and the project comes crashing down. Once the strategy is formulated, tactics can be employed, tested, changed. Short-term trade-offs may be required to advance the cause.

There is a false belief that compromise is morally flawed. Yet, the only political actor who doesn't need to compromise is the least moral of them all—the tyrant. All other politics has aptly been called "the art of the possible."

Followers can feel sold out by activists who settle for a compromise. Usually, they have not been sold out. They have had some of their demands traded for some of the demands of those on other sides of the issue. To convey this effectively, activists will need to use their political bilingual skills—speaking to the populace in its street-smart vernacular and to the government and elite circles in their in-group technocratic jargon. In supporting a leader committed to productive change or countering a leader misusing power, the activist circle cannot lose the populace to the prototyrant's information manipulation. Without support from the populace, the forces consolidating power for detrimental use will steamroll over the opposing activists' strategy and tactics, leaving them a faded memory.

Monsters exist, but they are too few
in number to be truly dangerous.
More dangerous are the common men, the functionaries
ready to believe and act without questions.

—PRIMO LEVI

Great activists are great question-askers. At their best, they ask the questions we in the populace should be asking but are too busy, insufficiently informed, or too plain tired to ask. In this sense, their role is to raise the quality of followership within the political system.

They invite us, and at times goad us, into thinking deeper about the consequences of the trajectory our leaders are taking us on. They ask us to consider if it is in our best interests to follow or if it is time to apply the brakes—to resist and search for or provide better leadership. In doing this, they perform a great service.

The Temptation of Violence

It is with regret, yet also a sense of moral urgency, that I must include a brief discussion of physical violence when discussing activists.

The essence of politics is providing nonviolent means to manage or resolve conflicting interests between groups of people.

Therefore, the use of violence to impose the will of one group on another is inherently a rejection of the political process.

The history of repressive regimes, on the right or the left, always includes an earlier stage in which gangs of armed supporters do the bidding of the emerging tyrant, physically silencing their opposition, effectively ending peaceful democratic processes. This was true in Rome after the fall of the republic and in every country in which some form of constitutional government was replaced or distorted into a dictatorial regime. In Europe, between the First and Second World Wars, this came to be represented by the infamous

Brown Shirts of Nazi Germany and the Black Shirts of Mussolini's fascist Italy. Simultaneously, the political left had its approximation in the Red Shirts of the Communist Militia of Germany and the Socialist Militia of Spain.[5]

Organized violent supporters are an extreme form of colluding followership that enables the prototyrant. Countering it requires the greatest courage on the part of those followers who may share a belief in that leader but who recognize there are legitimate and illegitimate ways of supporting them. It is the courage to not participate in the violent expression of that support despite intense implicit or explicit social pressures to do so.

Succumbing to the use of violence must be understood as crossing a line from activism to insurgency. Ironically, this choice might be justified to displace a tyrannical regime that has closed off all political avenues for creating change. It is a grave error to use it to install a regime when political avenues, though complex and frustrating, remain open.

If the political leader is encouraging violence as a type of "support," it is another red flag, as the violence becomes self-perpetuating. If you believe in that leader, demand that they and your fellow believers find *political* means of elevating them and their platform. Regardless of the sincerity of your passion or the intensity of social pressure, you are accountable for how you pursue the agenda. Be the courageous follower who holds the leader equally accountable.

ACTIVISTS	SUMMARY
Available Information	Movement messaging and specialized media
Incentives to Follow	Purposeful life, enacting a vision
Vulnerability	The blindness of the true believer
Risks	Persecution by the establishment, disapproval from the movement
Communication Channels	Social media followings
Courage Needed	Recognizing when backing the wrong leader
Power to Influence	Ability to shape messages/support positive leaders

CHAPTER 7

THE BUREAUCRAT

CIRCLE

The Arm of the Government Leader

.

"Bureaucracy is not an obstacle to democracy
but an inevitable complement to it."
—ECONOMIST J.A. SCHUMPETER

You may not be a government bureaucrat, but if you work in any type of hierarchy, you will still find this chapter relevant to your work. In any case, it will be helpful in understanding the behavior of bureaucrats at all levels of government who directly or indirectly affect your life.

Bureaucrats are a special class of followers.

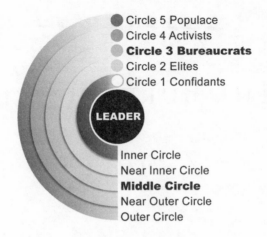

Circle 5 Populace
Circle 4 Activists
Circle 3 Bureaucrats
Circle 2 Elites
Circle 1 Confidants

LEADER

Inner Circle
Near Inner Circle
Middle Circle
Near Outer Circle
Outer Circle

The term *bureaucrat* has not fared well in popular culture, especially in recent years. It tends to be overlayed with images of poorly motivated, rule-bound functionaries who make life difficult when navigating the mundane requirements of society—tax payments, regulatory compliance, license renewals, immigration processes, and so on.

Yet, these same bureaucrats translate the vision and policies of political leaders into programs that affect the lives of citizens in crucial ways. Rather than a term of epithet, it would serve us better to understand the essential role bureaucrats play, how they may play it competently and beneficially, and what the nature of appropriate followership is in this role.

The number of bureaucrats in a large nation-state is nearly overwhelming. In a nation the size of the United States, the federal government operates with more than two million civilian personnel. Even this is dwarfed by the number of bureaucrats at lower levels of governance, including state and municipal, which approach five or six times that number. Many of these become specialists in their areas of expertise; some are world-class. Others become masters of making bureaucracy work despite its enormous size and complexity. Unlike bureaucracies that are staffed through patronage, all have a legitimate function to play in these highly complex, if often cumbersome, organizations.

The closer we get to observing the most talented individuals staffing these roles, the more we become aware of the depth of their knowledge and expertise. Yet, these highly qualified experts can become the channels for poorly thought-out policies and unintended adverse consequences.

A few years ago, I was conducting courageous follower training for a class of senior government managers. The concept of *courageous followership* suggests that to be effective at almost every level of an organization, individuals need to play both the leader and follower role adeptly. This offers a new model for the follower role that provides dynamic support for leaders but does not hesitate to speak truth to power. Nowhere is this more applicable than for government managers.

One of the managers in the class, a civilian woman employed by the United States Department of Defense, described her role in disposing of surplus military equipment. Rather than discard surplus or obsolete equipment, the US congress had passed legislation requiring the military to identify other ways it could be put to use. After all, the citizenry had paid for this equipment with their taxes, and contrary to common belief, conscientious civil servants keep in mind their obligation to minimize the waste of taxpayers' money. It seemed reasonable for the surplus equipment to be provided to state and municipal governments to use in their law enforcement agencies. Without much public debate or input, large amounts of armored personnel carriers and crowd control equipment began to be transferred to cities around the country. What could be bad about this?

UNINTENDED CONSEQUENCES

As we have come to see, this was not a policy that could be characterized as beating swords into plowshares. It resulted in the militarization of local police forces, very much at odds with "community policing" initiatives designed to create trust between law enforcement and those they are to protect. As cell phones began to capture the periodic misuse of lethal force by individual police officers—disproportionately against people of color—large-scale protests erupted across the land. It was only then, as a nation, that the citizenry began to see military-grade equipment being brought into the public square for crowd control. Suddenly, images of a militarized authoritarian presence suffused the national consciousness—in the language of this book, one might say a *prototyrannical ethos*. How had this come to be? Of course, I recalled the innocent description of this program that its manager had told the followership class.

The *Washington Post* noted, "During this summer's record-breaking nationwide Black Lives Matter demonstrations, some police have appeared ready for war. With armor, arms, and apparel resembling that of soldiers, they combatively disperse crowds, enforce curfews, and confront rioters.

Many police and sheriffs possess gear and equipment from or associated with the US armed forces. Some comes from the federal 1033 Program, which distributes excess military goods as federal grants-in-aid to police, sheriffs, and other agencies.

Based on our review of 1033 Program data from March 2020, we calculate that police departments in 49 percent of the approximately 1,000 places with protests as of June 8 have matériel from the 1033 Program. Of these, 160 police departments and a few county sheriffs received armored trucks, including MRAP vehicles, arguably the most prominent symbol of police militarization."[1]

THE CHALLENGE OF FOLLOWERSHIP
WITHIN BUREAUCRACY

The prior story is a graphic example of the unintended consequences of legislating any bureaucratic activity, but it is certainly not an isolated instance. Here, we get to the nub of the challenge of followership within the government bureaucracy. By law, bureaucracy is professionally bound to support and implement the policies of the nation's political leadership. In other words, to be conformist followers and, at times, colluders.

In democracies, political leaders are elected and then, presumably, pass or issue policies that align with the general will of the populace; in authoritarian regimes, this is less true, but there is an even greater expectation for the bureaucracy to refrain from behaving as independent actors.

When political leadership is relatively legitimate and policies are relatively equitable and purposeful, political theory and practice merge to serve the populace well. However, this relationship can be distorted in either direction.

If political leadership is significantly corrupt, a professional bureaucracy can attempt to mute its negative impact on the citizenry. In other words, to act as courageous followers, loyal to their oath of service. If the bureaucracy is entrenched and itself corrupt, its members can become colluders and amplify the corruption and ineptitude of the political leadership. If a political leader is seeking to reform government corruption or inefficiency, they may need to bring their personal charisma and persuasiveness directly to the populace to enlist its support in overriding entrenched bureaucratic fiefdoms.

Here, we see the various states of good and poor followership. A reformist leader may need to bring all their talents to bear in order to get resistant followership to perform its rightful role. Followership based on ethical values may need to exercise its talents to extract more competent and principled performance from its governing leaders. As the focus of this book is on how followers can identify leadership with autocratic tendencies and interrupt the potential progression toward a tyrannical regime, we will give our attention to that scenario, the challenges to overcome it, and the available tools for doing this.

THE PROBLEM OF MANY HANDS

In the prior story of repurposing military equipment for domestic policing, the mid-level manager did not appear to have any concerns or qualms about the role she was playing. It comported with the generally held value of not wasting taxpayer money. It was an approved program that came down the usual channels. In bureaucratic terms, it was quite legitimate.

What other ways can we look at this to explore the follower role in this crucial middle circle between government leaders and the people they are presumably there to serve?

Social scientists are aware of the problem of diffuse accountability, sometimes referred to as "the problem of many hands." A typical policy, program, or any formal initiative and the budget supporting it passes through many layers of approval. In a busy, deadline-driven environment, it is often easier to sign off on the initiative at your level than to begin to question it, which is likely to generate more meetings and paperwork. Even if you have a niggling discomfort, it seems reasonable to assume that if something is actually wrong with it, someone else will notice and take appropriate action. Of course, if everyone works on this assumption, then no one takes responsibility for the outcome of that decision chain. Often, this is how a bureaucracy will make a decision that no individual in that bureaucracy would have made were they the sole responsible party. I know this is a bit frightening.

There is another, perhaps more worrisome social dynamic that occurs that compounds the risk. In an earlier book on intelligent disobedience, I discussed a variation of the famous

Stanley Milgram obedience experiments in which 90 percent of the subjects continued participating in an experiment to its conclusion, which involved (or so they thought) giving 450-volt shocks to another human being with a heart condition. Of all the variations Milgram did on the obedience experiments, this is the one that produced the highest level of inappropriate compliance. What was different about it?

In the basic experiment, the subject read a question to the learner, marked the answer as right or wrong, and administered a shock if it was incorrect. The subject was led to believe that the learner was the subject, which they were not. Nor were they receiving actual shocks, though the simulation was very convincing. In that basic experiment, a disturbing two-thirds continued administering shocks all the way through 450 volts. That, of course, is and should be very disturbing. Milgram created varying social conditions to reduce this level of obedience in which that ratio came down to near zero. So why was this variation producing close to 100 percent obedience?

Instead of having the subject ask the question, mark the answer, and administer the shock, these tasks were divided between three people. Two were confederates of the researcher. The one who was not a confederate—the true subject—was simply asked to read the question to the learner. They were not, themselves, administering a shock. So what harm were they doing? Plenty, of course.

By remaining silent and cooperative, they were normalizing the outrageous act of continuing to raise the level of shocks being given to another human being despite that individual's protests and insistence that the experiment be stopped. The way the experiment was choreographed, they didn't even know if the "learner" was still alive as the shocks were increased to levels above 360 volts. They were able to tell themselves that they weren't giving the shocks and hold themselves blameless.

How few in a bureaucracy actually pull the trigger? The well-meaning, mid-level manager in my class was not driving a military vehicle into a crowd of demonstrators. She was not lobbing tear gas and wasn't dressed in the riot gear the local police used. She looked like the thousands of government managers who sit in a cubicle or small office and was rather proud of the work she was doing.

Suppose we tweak this scenario a bit and have a pro-totyrant use violence to quell democratic protests against increasing oppression. In that case, we see the passive role that the legions of bureaucrats under his authority play while he methodically consolidates power. By the time the bureaucrat wakes up to the way in which they are enabling that trajectory, it is often too late to stop the juggernaut, short of sabotage and self-sacrifice.

INCENTIVES TO FOLLOW AUTOCRATIC POLICY

The path of least resistance for the bureaucrat is to implement the policy that political leadership sets and follow orders on how to do so. This is almost always the safe course of action for the bureaucrat's career and their livelihood.

There is an old saying in Washington, DC, about

politicians and bureaucrats and the public they are there to serve: "A politician is someone who hates to say 'no'; a bureaucrat is someone who hates to say 'yes.'" This contains a grain of truth in that it is rare to be disciplined for sticking rigidly to the letter of a policy or order and easy to be criticized for exercising independent judgment.

Like most things, this fact of bureaucratic life can be functional or dysfunctional depending on context, interpretation, judgment, and culture. All senior executives in bureaucracies have been driven to despair by someone below them in the chain of command who is a stickler for the "letter of the law." At times, a sensible application of a rule requires flexibility to adapt the spirit of the rule to the circumstances. At other times, this stubborn "underling" actually holds an important ethical line.

Depending on culture, laws, and customs, bureaucrats have a range of incentives for complying with policies and orders. In cultures with weak private sectors, government employment is one of the few reliable paths to creating a financial floor for the family. In others, where there are robust entrepreneurial sectors, those who self-select into government service are typically more risk-averse or public service–minded—sometimes both. In cultures with fewer social safety nets, the benefits of a government position often include highly valued paid leave, health insurance, pension benefits, and other perks the employee values and may fear losing by "bucking the system." In cultures where the autocrat is already demonstrating no compunction about using brute force, failure to comply may incur much more severe penalties.

And yet, the bureaucrats whose choices feel constrained by these potential consequences often have an equally strong sense of loyalty to the people they serve, to the law or constitution, and to their conscience. These values compete with the incentives to "fall in line" and must either be honored or repressed with whatever psychological or physical consequences that choice brings.

PRINCIPLED DISOBEDIENCE

There is always a choice when faced with a values conflict. In a bureaucracy, one can refuse to implement an illegal order and risk the repercussions. What are the human costs of disobedience? It's easy to stereotype bureaucrats and make them into a symbol of "big government." But they are very much flesh-and-blood beings with the same concerns we have for health, family, financial solvency, a secure retirement, and so on.

There are practical steps one can take to soften the blow of potential reprisals for noncompliance with orders that violate civic values. But it is difficult to insulate oneself fully. Rational decision-making collides with courageous follower values, often leaving the bureaucrat with limited choices for working within the system to counter encroaching authoritarianism. Let's look at one example told to me by the former head of a whistleblower protection organization.

As we have seen, context is a large determinant of leader and follower behaviors. When countering external threats, governments will tend to become more autocratic, which, unchecked, can move them along the continuum to a dictatorial mode. After the 9/11 terrorist attacks on the United States in 2001, there was a great sense of urgency to prevent future attacks. This required plugging the intelligence gaps that had allowed planning for that attack to go undetected.

In this atmosphere, the administration of President George W. Bush, through the National Security Agency (NSA), which was charged with monitoring foreign communication for early warning signs, began bumping against and then crossing the boundaries permitted by law for monitoring US citizens. Executive orders were issued by the administration for what became known as "warrantless wiretapping"—in other words, forgoing the constitutional requirement for a court-approved warrant before initiating invasive searches of a suspect's property or communications.

At different points, several government bureaucrats became aware of this and felt duty-bound to uphold the law. One of them was Thomas Drake, a senior executive with the NSA. Drake helped to develop ThinThread, a program that monitored telecommunications and detected patterns of connections between likely terrorist nodes without scooping up metadata from US area codes, which would have violated the Espionage Act against spying on US citizens. It was estimated that ThinThread could have been developed and deployed for under $40 million.

Drake was initially confused by the lack of interest in Thin-Thread by higher-ups. He then discovered the NSA already had an arrangement to gather intelligence by listening to phone calls, which was costing vastly greater sums. This program, initially called Trailblazer and later Stellar Wind, was being carried out by executive order in violation of the constitutional requirement for court-approved warrants. Unlike ThinThread, it removed the protections against harvesting metadata from US citizens.

Trying and finding no way to remedy the matter within the agency or through congressional and judicial channels, Drake became a whistleblower and spoke with an accredited journalist about the NSA's violations, being careful not to disclose classified information. Despite this caution, he lost his security clearance and career and faced financially ruinous legal costs.

The example that was set by the administration ruthlessly attacking him when confronted with their illegality led a future whistleblower to avoid this risk by going straight to the press to reveal additional violations of the law. He, too, had his career and life severely interrupted.

By then, some of the highest-ranking political appointees could no longer countenance renewing the illegal warrantless wiretapping. They threatened to resign if this were done. When President Bush learned of this, he astutely supported his senior appointees, and the matter was sent to Congress to write constitutionally supportable legislation. The trajectory to potential tyrannical surveillance of American citizens was successfully interrupted.

The lesson I take from this is that the events leading to restoring legality by the government, occurred because a few courageous bureaucrats stepped up and did the right thing despite the risks and consequences. They acted as coura- geous followers, and they did so in the window before power could be further consolidated around the abuse of power.

An even healthier state would be for senior bureaucrats and political appointees to create a culture in which *internal* whistleblowing is treated as a courageous and loyal act, eliminating the need for *external* whistleblowing and its painful consequences. If you are one of these senior gov- ernment executives, this is not rhetorical musing but rather an invitation.

Create an organizational culture in which it is expected that those discovering violations of safety, legality, or human decency will call them out in a time and manner that min- imizes political embarrassment and allows for responsible remediation. This is courageous followership at its best.

CHAIN OF COMMAND AND COMMUNICATION CHANNELS AVAILABLE TO THE BUREAUCRAT

Let's further examine the actions to be taken when a bureau- crat has found the courage to rise above the incentives to remain compliant despite personal risks. They allow the moral conflict being experienced to ripen rather than deny or rationalize it. They recognize they have a choice of whether or not to follow increasingly autocratic leadership, even if that choice is difficult.

Knowing they must "choose their battles," they have decided the situation in question is a battle worth fighting. Perhaps lives are at risk or public health, or children's wel- fare, or national security, or public integrity, or constitutional safeguards that are being eroded intentionally or not by the regime. Do you see what serious issues our often disparaged bureaucrats may be dealing with in addition to the mundane? These are not "small potatoes."

Now, the nature of bureaucracy itself must be confronted. One of the ironclad rules of bureaucracy, whether written or unwritten, is respecting the chain of command. Skipping over one's direct managerial superiors is a cardinal sin, and this same chain of superiors are the very ones who can make or break the bureaucrat's career. Remember that everyone in that chain of command above them is also a follower and a civil servant with personal concerns about what they can lose if they fall out of favor with higher-ups and political appointees.

When I conduct courageous follower training for mid-level and senior career bureaucrats, I use an exercise to expose the dilemma this bureaucratic norm can produce. I introduce a hypothetical that requires them to wrestle with the cultural taboo of skipping channels. It is not a situation that involves a prototyrant but a more mundane example of a bad order coming down through channels. Still, it offers an opportunity to examine and test their values in the face of this rigid bureaucratic norm.

I create a scenario in which a lower-level government employee reports to a supervisor, who reports to a manager. These are three tiers within a larger bureaucratic system. The manager has instructed the supervisor to have their team take on additional responsibilities to their core function without providing extra resources. To make this matter consequential, let's assume this change jeopardizes public health or safety if done without the full resources safety requires. The team discusses this, explores different ways they can successfully implement the order, and concludes it cannot be done without serious failure of their core responsibilities. They inform their direct supervisor, who is *not* a courageous follower, and tells the team to just do the best they can despite the fact they will fail. What should the team do?

The class works in groups of four or five to develop responses to the situation. Many are clever or heroic in their attempt to get the job done, but the condition of the exercise is that the order cannot be successfully implemented—it is fundamentally flawed due to under-resourcing.

Some conclude they should suggest to the direct supervisor that he tell the manager the impending consequences. The problem with that approach is that the supervisor is intimidated by this manager and declines to do so. I have conducted this exercise with hundreds of seasoned bureaucrats and, to my recollection, almost none suggest going to the higher level manager themselves. Such is the power of the bureaucratic culture.

I then ask another question: If they were the senior manager, would they want to know if the order was unachievable so they could modify it while there was still an opportunity to find a successful alternative? Nearly 100 percent say yes, they would want to know. If so, wouldn't a manager two levels above them also want to know? At that point, they see the contradiction between the internalized cultural rule and their responsibility.

FINDING SOLUTIONS THAT MAINTAIN RESPECT FOR THE CHAIN OF COMMAND

The exercise then becomes how they can use language to frame the act of going above the supervisor's head while minimizing the damage this does to the relationship with that supervisor. The answers prove surprisingly easy once the cultural taboo is moved aside. To the supervisor, they can say something to this effect:

"We have too much respect for you to go behind your back. We can do this any way you prefer. You can come with us. You can let us take the risk and go on our own. You can even distance yourself from what we are doing if you think it is inappropriate. The only thing we can't do is leave the manager in the dark about the failure we believe will occur."

This is *not* asking for permission, which can be denied. They are acting on the value that the manager has a right to know about the likely consequences to make adjustments and avoid a mission failure. Depending on the supervisor's level of security or insecurity, they may hold this against the channel skipper, or they may not. Oddly enough, some research shows that in about a quarter of the instances, going to the next higher level *improves* the relationship with the supervisor for a variety of reasons, including having taken the problem off their hands.

When the individual follower or team goes to the higher level manager, how they phrase the information is important. They do not disparage their supervisor. They focus on the data and its predicted impact on the mission. In most cases, the manager will be grateful for the early warning unless there is a hidden political agenda. The next time they see the supervisor, they may even compliment them for having such an alert team!

But what about delivering messages that can make actors at an even higher level than the manager look bad? Now, the ante has been raised.

COMMUNICATING WITH HIGHER LEVELS

Because of the complexity of motivations in the first circle of followers (the confidants of the political leader), those in the second and third circles need to be particularly strategic in what information they feed to these agenda-driven, powerful followers who see their future inextricably linked to the autocratic leader. If they are found to be withholding information that would be of value to this first circle of followers, it could cost them their position. If they unartfully convey the information, they can be sidelined or scapegoated.

When possible, followers in the bureaucratic circle should frame the information in ways that promote the leader's legitimate self-interest (such as succeeding in the position) and serving the mission. Also, present the information so that it promotes a positive work culture. What does this look like? It is about avoiding the temptation of framing information in ways they believe ingratiate them to the first circle by sensationalizing it or inflaming its negative aspects. The very senior appointees to whom they send that information rarely have time to closely examine and vet the information they are given. Therefore, they may latch onto incendiary bits, which then come out in speeches and policies that only worsen conditions. Let's see how this might work.

In the US system of government, cabinet members are nominated by the president and confirmed by the Senate. Most of the senior staff that report directly to them are classified as political appointees rather than as civil servants, and their appointment begins and ends with each new administration. The political appointees who come in with a new administration are often highly critical of career employees, buying into the negative stereotype surrounding government workers. This results in knowledgeable and effective senior civil servants enduring a period of distrust with the new administration until they have demonstrated their true value. This usually occurs after the civil servants save the political appointees' bacon by helping them weather a public crisis. Here is an example of how cynicism needed to be countered by a career bureaucrat as it seeped into Circles 1 and 2 above her.

The new cabinet secretary was a confidant of the new president but highly cynical about the federal workforce. One of the political appointees who reported to him about the workforce played into that cynicism. Morale in the department was bad, and this appointee's approach to changing it was more or less "the beatings will continue until morale improves." Based on the assumption that the civil service was trying to make sure the new president failed, he designed performance review criteria that reflected this,

continued

thinking it would appeal to the cabinet secretary's cynical views. Naturally, this only worsened morale.

During this period, my client, who had been highly valued by the former administration, had to keep a low profile while she soldiered through, getting the job done. After a few months, by reason of her excellent work and her political astuteness, she came to the cabinet secretary's attention as someone to trust. Federal employees do an annual morale survey. His department wasn't looking good in comparison to others. Therefore, he didn't look good.

My client took the opportunity to explain to him the pride that civil servants take in their work. With her help, he began acknowledging this in his internal communication with the department's employees, and the surveys soon reflected this in the levels of morale reported. Now, tough news could be reported without cynicism and focus on the options for dealing with complex issues in productive ways. This avoided rash policy decisions being made on information from manipulative political followers.

Effective, ethical followers make the information that they are conveying to senior leaders as concise and digestible as possible. They frame it so the superior sees how that information is important to the mission, as well as to their reputation and their own boss's political capital. They highlight ways in which it can be used to persuade the most senior leader to make choices that are achievable, given existing conditions. Or to help them understand why a poorly conceived position should be rethought.

This is exemplary followership: remaining mission-centered while finding the leverage points that align the perspectives of those within the organization system for better outcomes.

COURAGE

Clearly, these carefully thought-out approaches are not guarantees of success when attempting to temper authoritarian impulses. But neither are they adding fuel to the fire. If a courageous follower is shrewd enough in their advice, and the higher-ups benefit from their counsel, they may be better positioned to be a moderating voice. At least one is trying to do the right thing and "living another day" to continue trying.

As bureaucrats rise in their organization, they may find themselves as little as two degrees of separation from the inner sanctum. With courage and skill, at the crucial point, they may indeed make a difference in the trajectory of the administration's use or abuse of power. Even at much lower levels, principled acts of courage make a difference.

Unlike water, courage can flow uphill to where it is needed. Courage modeled from below is as powerful as courage modeled from above.

In my workshops, I invite participants to identify their sources of courage. Often, it is an individual, historic or contemporary, who lived courageously. These personal role models come from all areas of their lives and are powerful touchstones. These can include you, who show the courage to take that principled stance.

Of course, it's one thing to influence your boss or their boss in a hierarchy to make the right decision. It's quite another to strategically exert influence that gets the head of government to change course. At best, it's a long shot, probably a bank shot involving several others closer to the leader—a matter of two or three degrees of separation.

Followers in this circle need to tap into and develop skills of strategic influence. The practice field available to them is their level of the governing system and a level or two above them. Conscious practice and experience may equip the bureaucratic follower to make that long shot if the window for doing so presents itself as part of a task force or an inquiry on which they are seated. A classic example of such a role was the Vietnam Study Task Force, which we will examine in Chapter 14 on coalitions of followers. It utilized a number of government bureaucrats to evaluate the US position, prospects, and policy in Vietnam while the war was being prosecuted with large numbers of casualties. Opportunities happen, and, like Scouts, it's good to be prepared.

Similar to operating a shipping canal in which water does, at times, "flow" uphill, it requires opening and closing strategically located "locks" to lift vessels of influence over obstacles in the terrain. In the next chapter, we will examine the skills for exerting positive bureaucratic influence that can provide this lift.

CHAPTER 8

THE BUREAUCRAT

CIRCLE

Developing Political Savvy

.

"Political, Savvy, or Astuteness:
Showing ability to understand diverse interest groups
and power bases within organizations and the wider
community, and the dynamic between them, to more
effectively achieve the public mission you serve."
—NATIONAL HEALTH SERVICE INSTITUTE,
United Kingdom

If a member of the bureaucracy cannot exercise the art of political savvy, it is unlikely they can make a difference in thwarting prototyrant orders and programs.

What are some of the elements to pay attention to and, if possible, master?

HOW POLITICAL IS TOO POLITICAL?

If an individual is acting "too political," we tend to mistrust them. We view their actions as self-serving and manipulative. In this context, we tend to define *political* as working only for one's own advantage and self-interest and not for a group or its mission. As in most things in life, it is a matter of degree. There is nothing wrong with self-interest as long as it stays in balance with the interests of the group.

In organizational life, political skills are also needed to advance the group's welfare. There is a spectrum of how individuals perceive and act within the system. This is generally thought of as *political astuteness* or *savvy*.

At one end of the political savvy continuum are those who operate purely on principle. They focus on the accuracy of the data relevant to their assigned work and on its unbiased analysis. Politics be damned. As a result of this approach, they are often frustrated by the failure of the leader or system to make use of their hard-won work product.

At the other end of the continuum are those who pay attention to the power relations in the system. They frame their information so those with the power to support or block initiatives take interest in their findings and are made into allies who support their recommendations. They are exercising political savvy and are effective at getting things done.

The higher one goes in a bureaucratic system, the more necessary it is to exercise political savvy to be effective or even survive. But political savvy without integrity can, and often does, have harmful consequences. Therefore, there is a desirable balance somewhere between the two polarities of the continuum, where an individual is acting on data with integrity while factoring in the political realities to accomplish what is needed.

Tackling the difficult and dangerous attempts to interrupt an autocrat's misuse of the bureaucracy rests on a foundation of political savvy.

BUT WHAT IS POLITICAL SAVVY?

You can think of political savvy as an athlete who is aware of every person's position on their team and the competing team, whether they are defending or attacking. They are alert to which direction other players are headed and where they will be in the next few seconds; where the ball, puck, or frisbee will be in those seconds; what the rules governing their moves are; and what maneuvers are available to them given their relative strengths and skills. Whew! Political savvy is an art that requires nearly comprehensive "field awareness."

As if that wasn't sufficiently challenging, if the object is to check an emerging tyrant, additional calculations are needed regarding your safety, protections available to you, contingency plans if those fail, and even escape plans. You can see why both courage and savvy are crucial.

In the normal course of events, political savvy at lower levels of government is not going to stop an emerging tyrant. Yet, when these skills are cultivated at those levels, they become available in situations in which bureaucrats may unexpectedly find themselves in a position to make a difference at higher levels.

Organizations tend to be fractal. What *fractal* means is

that systems tend to be self-replicating at different levels of scale. The culture lower down in a bureaucracy tends to have similar characteristics to those in higher levels of bureaucracy. Therefore, examining and applying political savvy where you are will make you more effective in your current position and better prepared for a once-in-a-career opportunity that may arise for influence in your field near the top of the food chain. This makes political savvy worth examining in some detail before we again look at how it may play out in thwarting the trajectory of a prototyrant.

TEACHING POLITICAL AWARENESS AND SAVVY

At one point, I worked with a remarkable senior manager in the US federal government. In that hierarchy, job rankings begin at level 3 and go up to level 15 for senior managers and directors. Above that is the highly selective Senior Executive Service (SES), which numbers about seven thousand out of more than two million federal personnel. This manager began her career as a GS 3 and worked her way up to SES—a rare feat! She had no advanced degrees, though a significant number of PhDs reported to her. Our close work with her revealed that she was not a ruthless individual who climbed the bureaucratic ladder on the backs of others; in fact, she was highly regarded by both peers and subordinates. She was committed to developing the talent two and three levels below her and retained my group to assist in this.

WHAT WAS HER SECRET?

One of her requests of us was to create a program to teach political savvy. She recognized how crucial it was and had not found an in-house resource for doing so. Accepting this assignment, I requested to interview her. Clearly, she, herself, had a significant amount of political savvy to have risen to the level she had, which ultimately was head of an agency with eight thousand employees.

Political savvy displays itself in two primary venues—group settings and one-on-one. In some ways, one-on-one is the easier dynamic. You pay attention to the interests of the other individual, both what they are trying to achieve within the mandate of their official role and their perceived self-interest for their career and life. This subject is reasonably well covered in my book *The Courageous Follower*. However, I had not previously explored the dynamics as they applied to group settings.

I asked this client for an hour of her time. When we sat together, I spread a large sheet of paper in front of us and asked her what I thought was a simple question: When she walks into a meeting, what does she pay attention to? We filled up the sheet of paper with an extraordinary number of elements that were in her field of awareness. After about forty-five minutes, she sat back, stunned: She had no idea of how many things she intuitively paid attention to in those settings that allowed her to navigate the diverse perspectives and interests successfully! She had unpacked many of the elements of political savvy in action before our eyes.

I organized this complex map into more digestible categories for the purpose of isolating the factors requiring
attention. We found this template could be applied in three
ways: to meeting participants from her organization, to participants from other organizations who needed to be brought
aboard or at least kept from hampering the objectives, and,
most surprisingly, to herself as a political actor.

I am including distillations of these charts. They help
isolate what you may need to give greater attention to in
developing political savvy. The first chart can be applied to
your agency or an interagency setting. Below the chart, you
will find a brief explanation of each of the categories. If you do
not work in a bureaucracy, you will still recognize situations
in which this awareness will be valuable in getting support
for a new idea or initiative in any group setting. In this sense,
we are all political actors.

Field of Political Awareness

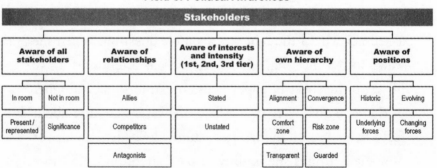

Stakeholders									
Aware of all stakeholders		Aware of relationships	Aware of interests and intensity (1st, 2nd, 3rd tier)	Aware of own hierarchy		Aware of positions			
In room	Not in room	Allies	Stated	Alignment	Convergence	Historic	Evolving
Present / represented	Significance	Competitors	Unstated	Comfort zone	Risk zone	Underlying forces	Changing forces
		Antagonists		Transparent	Guarded		

Awareness of Stakeholders

Stakeholder is a relatively contemporary word that acknowledges the complexity of systems surrounding any organization. It refers to anyone or any group that has an interest in the process and its outcome. Stakeholders can be members of your group, other internal departments, external organizations, and any of their constituencies. These all have the potential to become natural allies, rivals, or opponents.

Who is in the room tells you about the importance each group of stakeholders gives to the issue. The higher the rank or greater the expertise of the representative it sends, the more likely this issue is important to that group. In authoritarian cultures, one notices what degree of "hard-liner" has been sent to monitor the process and forcefully move it in a predetermined direction.

Who is *not* in the room requires even greater political awareness. Does this mean the issue is unimportant to them, or that they were not invited, or was there simply a schedule conflict? Equally important, does the absence of certain stakeholders infer any explicit or implicit biases or manipulation by the prototyrant?

Awareness of Relationships

What are the relationships of the people in the room *on this issue*? Political alliances shift with perceived self-interest. Who are natural allies on this issue? Who views themselves as competitors for territory, budget, or credit? Who are antagonists, either because of what is at stake or because of prior bad history? In an authoritarian culture, are there antagonistic rivalries that can be carefully leveraged to mute harmful outcomes of policy decisions?

Awareness of Interests and Intensity

In politics (or war), it is not always the group with the most numbers and resources that prevails. At times, it is the group that has the most to lose and pulls out all stops to avoid being annihilated. Which of these stakeholders views the issue as existential to their survival? Which view it as important but secondary, and which as only peripheral to their core interests? Assessing this can help adjudicate which alliances to make and the chances for outcomes other than that being urged by the dominant leader or group.

Awareness of One's Hierarchy

These are all the people above you in the chain of command who hold positional power, whether they are at the table or not. Holding their perspectives in mind helps you maximize "the running room" you have to achieve the expected objective while avoiding landmines. These are some of the elements to pay attention to in this column of the chart:

Alignment versus Divergence
Politics operates at every level of an organization. Some degree of politics is natural in a relatively free culture and

still covertly operates when suppressed by an autocrat. To the degree one can ascertain this, how aligned are senior levels of leadership on the issue at hand? Are there divergences at senior levels that can provide room for maneuvering at your level?

Awareness of Issue Positions

It is important to determine what the comfort zone of others is—particularly those above you in the hierarchy. Where do they see the boundaries of what is acceptable to negotiate or even discuss; what do they consider sensitive, confidential, or too high risk due to threats it may present to their position or power? Being alert to this can prevent missteps that weaken your influence.

Transparent versus Guarded

How transparent can you be on this issue in this setting? Are you free to put all the data and intentions on the table, or would that be naive and weaken and erode your leadership's trust in you? In an authoritarian culture, transparency can be viewed as "soft" or disloyal or make you vulnerable to retribution before you have built a strong enough position to withstand this.

Awareness of Positions

Different factions come to the meeting with positions they are defending or holding as desired outcomes. They may vary widely from your own. Understanding these will help you factor them into your strategy and maybe into modifying your near term objectives.

Historic and Evolving

What have been the historic positions of all parties on the issue at hand? The history and complexity often get lost with time and changes in personnel. Become deeply informed on the issues so the leaders you are trying to influence cannot discount you as being uninformed. Understand the nuances and complexities of the positions so you can help the leaders freshly see the fundamentals.

Underlying Forces and How They Are Changing

What factors contributed to those historic positions? The big trends—political, economic, social, technological, environmental—and the ones narrowly and deeply relevant to the existing position and the leader's impulses? How have those factors changed, and are they on a trajectory to change further? How may these suggest acceptable alternatives for addressing the issues with less brinkmanship than the leader is heading toward?

Awareness of Other Hierarchies

This will become another column on the chart if other agencies or constituent groups are involved in the issue. When I interviewed my client, I found that for all the attention she gave to the dynamics within her agency, she asked the same questions of other agencies and groups who had overlapping jurisdictions or interests. One significant difference is that she was not in a position to get as much information about the others as she was about her own. We added these factors in the column for other stakeholder hierarchies:

Awareness of Information

Don't Know

Given the topic at hand, what is thought to be known about the information on which other stakeholders are operating, and what is not known but relevant?

Must Know

Are there some things that must be known in order to be prepared adequately? How can that information be acquired? What research can be done from public documents? Which allies might have knowledge of or access to nonpublic information?

Can't Know

What simply can't be known? What are the most probable scenarios that could act as surprises in the meeting? How can we prepare to respond to those scenarios?

Awareness of Own Political Situation

While good bureaucrats are professional and place their official responsibilities above their personal political preferences, they are still political actors in the organizational scheme. In the same meeting, my client mapped out her self-awareness in any political setting. This was particularly astute of her. The elements we captured follow.

Field of Political Awareness — Self

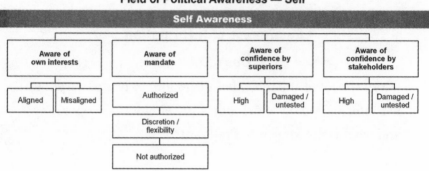

Awareness of Own Interests

If we are alive, we have interests. Ideally, professionals manage them to keep the organization's mission central to their focus. Nevertheless, organizational changes can affect the projects about which we are passionate as well as impact our careers. It is healthy to maintain awareness of how our interests are aligned or not to the leadership's priorities.

In the usual push and pull of bureaucratic life, one uses a sense of professionalism and personal ethics to strike an appropriate balance between one's interests, the leader's, and the organization's. In an autocracy that is veering toward tyranny, both alignment and misalignment are problematic and require careful consideration.

If our perceived self-interest is aligned with the autocratic trajectory, a personal values review is in order. Are we being suborned in ways we will come to regret?

If our mission-based interests appear aligned with the autocrat, though not with their means of achieving them, how do we take advantage of the autocrat's power without violating the values we hold dear?

If our interests and values diverge from the autocrat's, we will need to manage the nonalignment with great discretion, as we are at an inflection point with potentially irreversible consequences. Before we examine the navigation of these treacherous waters, let's continue to assess other factors.

Awareness of Mandate

By custom and role, the bureaucrat is operating as an agent of political leadership. They do not have carte blanche to create different goals and priorities. Awareness is needed as to what one is authorized to offer, negotiate, or approve and what one is not. Failure to be clear about this distinction will result in a loss of leadership's trust. In an autocracy, this can pose significant ethical strain. We will explore options for dealing with this as we examine these dynamics.

Awareness of Confidence by Superiors

If trust is high, the bureaucrat has leeway to make decisions within the general guidelines they have been given. One may have enjoyed high confidence under a former office-holder and mistakenly believed this trust transferred to the new relationship before it has been developed. Or, recent events may have eroded the trust that will need to be rebuilt. In an autocracy, this is particularly difficult if one is committed to minimizing the impact of the autocrat's methods or decisions.

Confidence of Stakeholders

Similar dynamics apply to the stakeholders with whom one is interacting. If trust has not yet been developed or has been compromised with those who will be affected by decisions, you will need to attend to this so that decisions are viewed as fair. In an autocratic ethos, this will be particularly difficult without betraying the stakeholders or being betrayed. Heightened alertness and the skill to walk a fine line are needed to serve as a check on the abuse of power.

Political Savvy as a Collaborative Practice

Despite the unsavory connotations many have with the concept of "being political," in fact, it is a very collaborative way of working. Why? Because it factors in the perspectives and perceived needs of others who are involved in the process and affected by its outcome.

Yes, political savvy can be used manipulatively. But it can also be used to satisfy as many interests as possible without disadvantaging one's interests any more than necessary. In this sense, it is an awareness and skill to be cultivated not only for its effectiveness but also for its potential to build productive relationships. In addition to this being good for its own sake, it is not incidental to our concern here with being able to interrupt the progression to tyrannical political leadership. Successful intervention almost always requires a coalition. Where trust has been built by paying attention to the interests of as many parties as possible, there is a stronger foundation for developing a coalition when needed.

All the elements of political awareness need to be brought to bear to know where there is political space to make a difference and where there is not. It serves bureaucrats well to raise their level of political savvy while remaining committed to their integrity and professional values.

A caveat is that no one can consciously hold all the elements of political awareness in mind as they develop their skills. It is better to focus on one or two at a time until they are integrated and then work on others. For instance, start with paying attention to who is in the room and what that means. When this becomes your established way of engaging in meetings on consequential subjects, go on to the next skill and work on that. Of course, if there is a hugely important meeting coming up, you can prepare for it by taking out these charts and thinking about each of the elements for that specific meeting.

IDENTIFYING AND ENROLLING ALLIES

Ultimately, a coalition will be needed to deflect or thwart the prototyrant's trajectory. The qualities that engender soft power can win allies who are not yet cowed by or committed to the prototyrant.

Those at the nonpolitical end of the spectrum, in which data, rationality, and principle are of primary importance, can make the mistake of relying on their unblemished record of commitment to values and purpose and the rationality of their argument to bring others around. They gape in dismay when this fails to win the day. The awareness and use of political dynamics are essential for convincing those who are swayable to support actions that contain the incipient abuse of power.

This can be a tall precipice to scale. We have seen the incentives for bureaucrats to play it safe, hew to policies and orders coming down through the hierarchy, and justify to themselves their lack of culpability for harmful outcomes. It requires the field awareness of a chess player who keeps the whole board in their mental map and identifies a strategy that can prevail despite a seemingly weaker position. When this skilled follower acts as a natural leader among peers, if others have the courage to support them, the chances of success are significantly improved.

How You Might Read a Room

The drafting committee of the Presidential Advisory Commission on Modernizing Executive Power was meeting to vote on the white paper Clara had been tasked with writing. It would not have binding force but would make public the most salient concerns of this diverse panel. Clara surveyed who would be in the room. Of the eleven people around the table, she needed at least five others to join her in support of the recommendations that would discourage a consequential consolidation of presidential power. She identified the best candidates.

Two-star general Alfonso Blackmon took great pride in defending underprivileged segments of the citizenry. She could appeal to his sense of justice.

Former senator Michael Malkovics was in the twilight of his long career of public service. His eye was on his legacy, which could be sealed one way or the other with his decision in this matter.

Judge Maya Robinson was a rising star, always looking for opportunities to define herself and broaden her potential constituency. She understood what was at stake.

The nationally respected Bishop Woods had become ill during the empanelment of the commission. He wanted to conclude the matter at hand and return to his home, where he could rest and be surrounded by family.

Secretary of Homeland Affairs Sheilagh MacDonald had an innovative agenda. She needed a more participatory political atmosphere to test her ideas and vision.

The Hon. Kingsley Winbush's family nursed a long-standing feud with the prototyrant, which could be leveraged.

Clara carefully prepared her arguments for the motion to approve this draft of the committee's recommendations. She fashioned them to highlight their centrality to the health of the democracy while bringing in perspectives that would sit well with the perceived self-interest of the

continued

potential majority votes needed to pass the initiative. She presented her case with confidence that it was as strong as possible, both on its merits and its sensitivity to what individual members of the committee would deem attractive.

Regardless of well-honed political savvy, bureaucrats will face significant hurdles in their attempts to apply the brakes to increasingly disturbing behavior. In the next chapter, we will look at some of the strategies when seeking to overcome these obstacles.

CHAPTER 9

THE BUREAUCRAT

CIRCLE

Navigating Dilemmas

·

"If they don't give you a seat at the table,
bring a folding chair."
—SHIRLEY CHISHOLM, the first African
American woman elected to Congress

CAN YOU SIT AT THE TABLE?

If you are going to make a difference in interrupting prototyrannical policies coming through your agency, it helps
to "have a seat at the table"—in other words, to be in the
crucial meetings where strategic decisions are debated and
to have a voice in those meetings.

Bureaucracies are deeply ingrained in their culture. A few smaller agencies may be relatively informal and invite input from all levels, even encouraging it. Large bureaucracies usually do not. Protocol, status, rank, and formality all play a role, which one deviates from at one's peril.

At very senior levels, the political players are often the only ones at the table. Their staff—the bureaucrats—are usually seated around the periphery of the meeting room. The protocol is that they only speak when invited to do so. Those with close relations to the political leaders work out acceptable ways of passing notes to keep their boss from looking inadequately briefed or from misspeaking in ways they will regret, and that the bureaucrats will need to clean up.

The Club de Madrid

The Club de Madrid is a rarefied club. Its hundred or so members are all former heads of state or heads of government of a democratic nation. Its charter calls for 80 percent of its members to come from countries that made the transition to democracy since 1975. I was asked to help design and facilitate a strategic planning retreat that was held in Prague. Two dozen former heads of state or government participated.

The secretary general of the Club de Madrid was a woman who had been the prime minister of Canada. She was responsible for leading and managing the staff and creating the capacity to help its members advise and support heads of government and state from emerging democracies.

She had spent many hours with her staff and me designing the retreat format and process.

The Club members sat around a large conference table. Simultaneous translators sat behind glass panels. The president of the club was a highly regarded former president of Brazil. He sat next to the secretary general. The dozen or so staff and I sat in chairs along the wall.

A former president of a Central American country voiced a disagreement with the secretary general on a point of strategy. Instead of allowing the conversation to play out, the president of the Club de Madrid shut down the dialogue and called for a special committee to review the matter. This smacked of the experience all too often reported by women in senior roles of being shut down at the table.

A brief recess was called. My client, the secretary general, was fuming at what she interpreted as having her authority undermined by her male colleagues. I moved to her side to help her safely vent and develop a strategy for when the meeting resumed fifteen minutes later. I felt like a trainer at a boxing match giving my bloodied fighter smelling salts and a pep talk before the next round began. We focused on getting the agenda back on track. Sometimes, those without a seat at the table need to use the space available to them to work with and through those who are at the table.

Even if you are seated at the table, you can easily be disinvited to future meetings if those higher up are displeased by their data being publicly challenged or if ideas you offer bleed support from their position. Yet, at times, if one doesn't speak up, decisions will be made on incorrect or incomplete data that are difficult or impossible to reverse.

If you are at the table, there is an art to speaking up at these junctures and framing the data or perspective in ways that do not make others at the table, particularly those of senior rank, look bad. One way of doing this is to frame the data as having just been received before the meeting, so they could not have been informed of it earlier. This saves face for the leader. Another tactic, when morally defensible, is positing a viewpoint as one who appears to support what the senior leaders at the table wish to achieve and, within the context of overall support, alerting them to downsides that may make them look bad. The astute leader can receive this as an act of loyalty, while the bureaucrat has deftly deflected damaging errors or tempered destructive excesses.

In the delightful book *Orbiting the Giant Hairball,* author Gordon MacKenzie warns that if we seem to represent views too far outside the organization's culture, we will not be viewed as useful to the organization.[1] In this case, we may be perceived as an external threat, causing the system to send out antibodies to neutralize us. We must astutely frame things within the language and culture of the organization to be perceived as "one of us," even as we nudge the dialogue in more beneficial directions that support core human values.

As we see, there is a balancing act between the benefits of speaking the truth as we see it and telling it in ways that do not get us disinvited from the table, where we can potentially make a difference. We can err in either direction: speak too forcefully and be disinvited from the table or remain silent and become a colluder in policies that should be questioned.

If we have been at the table for a considerable time without making a difference, we will need to acquire allies who are willing to speak up with us. Three senior female aides at the White House in Washington, DC, agreed to jump in to support each other when a point they were making was being dismissed before being given respectful consideration. Regardless of gender, if the pattern persists, find another table from which to counter the effects of policies and practices we deem unjust, unwise, or unlawful.

COUNTERING COLLUSIVE FOLLOWERS

We have examined the spectrum that runs from lesser to greater political savvy. In doing so, we see that paying attention to power relationships is necessary to be effective in complex systems, particularly political ones. The task is to do so without drifting far from a grounding in reliable data and principle. This presents a conundrum for the courageous bureaucrat.

In a prototyrannical atmosphere, those who become trusted by the tyrant are typically those with the least principle and the most willingness to do the tyrant's bidding. In meetings in which decisions are being made that will have an adverse effect on democratic institutions, the power will seem to reside with those who are unscrupulous and have earned the prototyrant's trust. While it is politic to avoid antagonizing these overly political participants as much as possible, it is, of course, a moral mistake to align with them. But how can we apply the model of political savvy if we do not align with those who have the favor of the leader? Here, we must examine the alternative sources of power as we navigate this treacherous political landscape.

Social scientists do well at describing various types of power, including what are called *legitimate power, coercive power, reward power, expert power,* and *the power of charisma*. I would add to these *reflected power*, which, for our purposes, is the power that an individual enjoys who is perceived to be close to the autocrat. Reflected power can be formidable but is not necessarily decisive while we are still in the window for potential intervention. There are other balancing sources of power that are not always given the recognition they merit. The power of reputation for integrity and trustworthiness is high among these. So is the power of courage and truth-telling. A history of service, risk, and having paid a personal price for loyalty to core values all earn respect and, thus, power to influence.

This is the bureaucratic version of soft power. Its version of hard power is the capacity to work the system to pass regulations, award contracts, or make appointments that reward individuals and groups who can serve as a check on the prototyrant's power grab. We can overestimate or underestimate our soft power. The tendency is to underestimate it, which then supports the "safer" course of not sticking out our neck. This is where courage comes in to fill the gap between the power we have and the power that is needed to make a difference. With the stakes as high as they are, if there is a chance to make a difference, the courageous follower takes that chance.

In the political world, we must be realists. But realism without principle is the precursor to tyranny. The savvy bureaucrat who marries principle and realism in proper proportion is the follower needed to preempt the prototyrant.

THE BUREAUCRAT'S DILEMMA WHEN DEALING WITH A CHARISMATIC AUTOCRAT

There is a dilemma the bureaucrat dealing with an autocrat may face. Leaders and followers always interact within a specific context. In democratic societies, the strongman or autocrat is typically elevated to an office in periods when the populace is experiencing social anxiety, economic uncertainty, or external threats. They are primed for the message of a charismatic autocrat who promises them easy answers to difficult problems and targets the existing government as the cause for inaction.

While the charismatic populist is using and inflating existing anxieties, there is often an element of truth to what they are saying. The people may be wondering why the government can't do something to ease their anxieties or deprivations. The government can, in fact, do so, but it rarely moves quickly and dramatically. Its established processes— some mandated by law, some by rules and regulations, others by custom—often require the input of many constituencies and coordination between a number of different agencies and layers of government. This requires meetings, hearings, comment periods, collaboration, compromise, and documentation, all of which take time and have an uncertain outcome.

A short-term value of the populist autocrat is that they do not hold themselves to these protracted processes. With little respect for diverse perspectives or conventional norms, they tear through the maze of obstacles and seek to ram through solutions. This is a two-edged sword. On one side of the blade, this cuts through cumbersome process and accelerates muscular responses to the oppressive conditions, earning the support of the populace. On the other side of the blade, ramming through solutions weakens the institutions designed to assign resources to programs and populations equitably. It opens the process to large-scale corruption that is difficult to document.

The principled bureaucrat is committed to preventing the undermining of institutions, but must be politically astute. It would be a mistake to thwart the need for action, which has the support of the populace. This is not a task that responds well to purists. The bureaucrat will need to walk the line to support rapidly easing the burdens of the populace while maintaining the integrity of institutions. Skill, judgment, and flexibility will be required to achieve this.

REFUSING ORDERS THAT VIOLATE HUMAN RIGHTS

The greatest responsibility for correct followership to political leaders resides in a special class of bureaucratic followers—the military, law enforcement, and intelligence services. There is a conundrum here. Those who serve in these authorized vehicles of state power must be willing to use force, and at times lethal force, at the command of legitimate political leadership, yet also need to be the most willing to disobey if the order is illegitimate.

In liberal democracies, the oath taken is to defend against all enemies of the constitution, internal and external. However, in the case of a de facto or actual coup, both sides will claim legitimacy regardless of objective reality. How will military personnel, intelligence, or law enforcement officers recognize the true defender from the usurper?

The usurper of political power violates the essential values that protect individual freedoms and collective decision-making. They do so supposedly in defense of the state, while undermining their very core. The classical meaning of the term *liberal values* must be understood and differentiated from attempts to distort and degrade its meaning. Classical liberal values are the sacrosanct protections of individual freedoms to think, speak, write, associate, congregate, and live free of arbitrary government coercion. The only legitimate constraints on these rights are where their use denies or abrogates the same rights for others.

Interestingly, these rights, conferred upon all human beings living within a society, are not fully given to the bureaucrats or the armed enforcers of the law and protectors of national defense. In those capacities, individual rights are subordinated to the constraints and responsibilities of the role they are serving. It would be chaotic if everyone in a government agency freely gave their opinion to the media on the correct interpretation of events, policies, and preferred strategies. Or if they were enforcing their interpretation of laws and regulations. There is merit to norms and rules that require government policy positions to be systematically developed, communicated, and executed.

At the same time, those *not* in official roles must be completely free to express their views, whether consonant with or contrary to the government's preferred position. It is the bureaucrat who must distinguish between their professional constraints and the populace's unfettered rights. Maintaining this distinction leads the bureaucrat to consequential moral junctures. If they draw a line against oppressive policies and orders, they risk losing their standing, their job, their career, or, in extreme cases, their life. Nonetheless, there is always an available moral choice. What we seek to do is make that choice unnecessary by staying alert to the progression of autocratic impulses and intervening early enough to prevent consolidating control of state power.

Professional training in these roles would ideally include exercises in which illiberal forces attempt to create confusion and usurp power. Public servants must be able to see through the fog of information war. They must be able to discern the true defender of a free system from the usurper, who always argues they are defending the system. Creating the capacity to make this distinction is prophylactic in a free society. Once authoritarians gain control of a bureaucracy, such training or conversation would be patently and forcefully prohibited. The following example is an important start in this direction.

The Royal Military Academy, Sandhurst

In 2017, I was invited to speak at the Royal Military Academy Sandhurst on courageous followership and intelligent disobedience. Though it does not offer academic degrees, Sandhurst is roughly the equivalent of West Point in the American system of training career officers and enjoys at least as much prestige. Five years later, the British Army incorporated the principles found in courageous followership and intelligent disobedience into the British Army Doctrine under the title "A British Army Followership Doctrine Note."

In November 2023, this doctrine was officially launched in a day-long symposium at the National Army Museum in London to a live and virtual audience of about five thousand participants, mostly from the British and NATO military.

The document is filled with excellent definitions and explanations of the values expected to be upheld when in the follower role. Point 47 of the twenty-two-page document includes the following explanation of intelligent disobedience:

"47. Intelligent disobedience entails the potential need and reasonable freedoms to contravene a direct order or instruction. This may be necessary where a follower is presented with new or conflicting information or a moral dilemma of which the leader is unaware or unable to be informed. In extremis, it can also relate to the actions of a follower who judges an order to be immoral, unethical, or

continued

unlawful. In such instances, the follower has an obligation to challenge such an order."[2]

Note that the follower doesn't only have the right to disobey an unlawful or immoral order; they have the obligation to do so.

Formal policies such as this clarify and strengthen the position of armed members of the bureaucratic apparatus to resist being misused to override democratic norms.

WHEN THE BUREAUCRAT IS NOT THE ONE PULLING THE TRIGGER

An unexpected dilemma can arise among bureaucrats who seem to be doing largely administrative or programmatic work. Imagine this scenario: You are an analyst for the US Department of Homeland Security. Your role is simply to analyze communication traffic and report suspicious patterns. This is quite an ordinary role for a protective force. You are doing your part in keeping the people of your nation safe from terrorist attacks.

A new regime has come to power. It is using the same methodology to identify communication patterns. But now, these are being used to detect political opposition that is protected by the constitution. An unease settles over your bureau. There are incidents of dissident media reporters being "disappeared" or having "accidents" from hotel balconies. You are certainly not involved in grabbing anyone off the street or pushing them out of windows. You are simply an analyst. Your hands are clean. You are doing the job you have always done, which allows your family to enjoy a comfortable life. Is this a moral problem?

Remember the disturbing research we reviewed earlier of a variation of Stanley Milgram's famous "shock machine" obedience studies. In this particular variation, the subject was only asked to read the question. Another individual was administering "the shocks." In that variation, *90 percent* of subjects obeyed, all the way to 450 volts. After all, they weren't personally administering the potentially lethal shocks! This reduced the psychological strain on them, so they went along with the attitude of a spectator rather than of an accomplice.[3]

Think of the tens of thousands of bureaucrats in analogous situations. They are not launching a killer drone at a supposed but questionable enemy vehicle, though they are providing coordinates or checking a ready-to-launch list. They are not separating a child from a migrant mother, though they may be maintaining a roster of occupants in the detention facility. They are not firing tear gas on a group of civil demonstrators, though they may have procured the armored vehicle from which the canister is launched.

This minimum level of psychological strain in performing their duties converges with the career incentives for implementing the program or executing the order. Thus, we create conditions in which normal human empathy is subordinated to following protocols whose outcome is not one's responsibility. Or so it seems. Therefore, we look back at historical events and ask, "How could they have done that?" Yet, we ourselves may also have done that in similar circumstances . . . and then needed to live with that passive collusion.

CULTURES THAT SUPPORT BUREAUCRATIC DISSENT

Naturally, it is easier if a bureaucrat is operating within a culture that provides some support for principled dissent. This does not make it easy to dissent, as informal group pressures are still operative. However, creating a policy basis for dissenting may bolster the willingness to do so when circumstances warrant dissenting voices. Examples of this exist in various institutions.

Similar to the British Army Followership Note, the US Military Code of Conduct requires personnel to obey all *legal* orders. This is read to mean that if a member of the military receives *illegal* orders, they are not required to obey and, indeed, can be found guilty of obeying if the order is deemed to be unlawful. This puts a great burden of responsibility on the individual soldier in presumably high-stress situations. But at least there is a legal framework to support principled action. Some military theorists argue that this same principle applies to *immoral* orders. Followers who act on a moral basis are on less firm legal ground but may be the true heroes.

The Singapore Armed Forces once created a video called "A Journey Into The Heart of Darkness." It used well-known images of widely agreed-upon war crimes from different parts of the world. It cautioned individual service members not to follow illegal or immoral orders that would perpetrate such crimes.

Courageous diplomats from nations all over the globe are honored for risking their careers in unauthorized actions that have saved the lives of persecuted minorities within a country. A number of these are honored in The Righteous Among the Nations database maintained by the Holocaust Memorial in Israel.

One of the more interesting examples of supporting dissent is found in the US Foreign Service, whose officers serve under the US Department of State. For the last half-century, the American Foreign Service Association has conferred awards for "Constructive Dissent" on personnel at each of four different levels of the service. Their intent is to encourage risk-taking and "the courage to dissent within the system."[4] The awards are presented at an annual event held within the Department of State. Note how this differs from "whistleblowing," which is more typically done outside the system.

The virtue of these and other efforts is in providing support for bureaucrats in sensitive positions who risk intervening in abusive autocratic behavior before it reaches a level at which it is nearly impossible to stand up to that behavior.

American Foreign Service Association Dissent Awards

The awards are for Foreign Service employees who have "exhibited extraordinary accomplishment involving initiative, integrity, intellectual courage and constructive dissent."

The awards publicly recognize individuals who have demonstrated the intellectual courage to challenge the

continued

system from within, question the status quo, and take a stand, no matter the sensitivity of the issue or the consequences of their actions.

The issue does not have to be related to foreign policy. It can involve a management issue, consular policy, or the willingness of a Foreign Service Specialist to take an unpopular stand, to go out on a limb, or to stick their neck out in a way that involves some risk. Nominees may or may not have used the formal dissent channel.

Yet it is even more important for bureaucrats who do not experience this type of organizational support to employ their integrity and political savvy to interrupt a toxic progression to tyrannical rule. It is for them that cultural honors like The Righteous Among the Nations serve the purpose of recognizing and rewarding acts by courageous individuals who take a stand and often pay a significant personal and professional price for doing so.

A worthy initiative for those in bureaucracies without a formal process for supporting courageous stances would be to work for the creation of one. When courageous moral stances are made at appropriate lesser moments, the courage muscle begins to develop for when it is needed to interrupt a power grab by a would-be political tyrant.

TO THWART OR SUPPORT?

Bureaucrats know there are a variety of tools that can be used to thwart policy changes or implementations. Morally, this is again a two-edged blade. If being used to delay or block patently immoral policies, one can argue the justifications for these tactics. But in a liberal democracy, this is also a problem. The government is elected to formulate policies. If this is done in reasonably fair, transparent, and lawful ways, it is not the place of the bureaucracy to thwart those policies.

But what about when the elected government operates in deceitful, secretive, and unlawful ways—in other words, as a prototyrannical government? What is the bureaucrat's responsibility?

If the politics are still largely democratic, the offending government can be turned out of office in the next election cycle. Bureaucrats aware of this may choose to slow-walk, stall, and delay policy approval or implementation to mitigate damage. The ethics of this can be argued, but the use of procedural power is part of the politically savvy tool kit. If the government retains power in a fair election, bureaucrats are faced with complying or, in egregious situations, resigning on principle. Continuing to sabotage the government undermines the representative government they are seeking to defend.

If the democratic political process has been eviscerated by an autocratic regime, reducing it to a mere fig leaf, how does the ethical equation change? While the outward norms of bureaucratic culture may need to be maintained as their own form of fig leaf, moral accountability rises to a first-order concern. It is in this situation that "just following orders" is itself a crime, and followership is tested at its moral core.

The military trials that followed the defeat of Nazi Germany in 1945, popularly known as the Nuremberg Trials, were conducted under the principles established in the charter of the International Military Tribunal. Article eight of the IMT Charter states, "The fact that the Defendant acted pursuant to order of his Government or of a superior shall not free him from responsibility, but may be considered in mitigation of punishment if the Tribunal determines that justice so requires."

Bureaucratic strategies for buffering the populace from the predation of the paramount leader and their cronies must be used with great dexterity. More fundamentally, courage must overcome the reality of personal risk; loyalty to the nation must overcome the temptation of material reward for ignoring abuses of power. Political savvy must combine with shrewd survival tactics, while strategy is developed and enacted by coalitions of those faithful to their democratic form of government.

It is in the window where the abuse of power is evident and documented, but before power is consolidated, the bureaucrat needs to act. Once power is consolidated, senior positions will be filled with cronies, adjudication processes will be nullified or packed with lackeys, media channels will be suborned or shuttered, and political opposition will be silenced. The bureaucrat may be in the best position to see the progression to tyranny from within and to sound alarms.

The more this can be done in full "sunlight," the harder it will be for the prototyrant to nullify principled bureaucrats.

Now, we are in the arena of whistleblowing, even if standard channels are followed to alert oversight bodies. The bureaucrat, acting as a defender of liberal democracy, threatens the illiberal autocracy. They must be prepared for retaliation. Minimally, this means lining up financial resources to sustain themselves and their family, and legal resources to stand with them in the face of attempts to discredit and silence them. It may mean taking far greater precautions for personal safety.

While Aristotle holds courage as a premiere virtue, he warns us that acting without any fear of consequences is rash and lacking in prudence. The bureaucrat is at the juncture where certain questions must be asked to distinguish between acts of courage and those of recklessness:

- Are the institutional channels still sufficiently intact that they can be used to report deep concerns about the abuse of power?

- If they are judged to be so, is it prudent to use them before considering further options?

- If those channels are no longer to be trusted or have been used to no effect, what powers remain to check the progression of the prototyrant?

- Who in your field of awareness is best positioned to help thwart the danger?

- What is the best way to approach them, and what is the evidence and argument on which they are most likely to act?

In the worst cases of progression to tyrannical rule, bureaucrats themselves can only buffer the effects on the populace but cannot themselves transform or displace the prototyrant. Doing so will require a coalition, ideally involving all circles of followership but minimally involving well-placed elites and activists with the power to wake the populace to the danger in front of their eyes.

We will examine the nature of these coalitions in a later chapter devoted to this crucial coordinated activity. Meanwhile, the bureaucrat who has played it safe in their career is thrust into a moral role that is anything but safe. Their core principles, tightly interwoven with political awareness, are needed if they are to walk with their head held high (and still attached) through the minefield being lain by the prototyrant.

Taking the liberty to degenderize the words of the great playwright, political dissident, and former president of the Czech Republic, Václav Havel, they remain highly salient:

The real test of an individual is not how well they play the role they invent for themselves but how well they play the role destiny assigned to them.

—Václav Havel

BUREAUCRATS	SUMMARY
Available Information	Political appointee briefings, data agency collects
Incentives to Follow	Organization inertia, job retention, chance to make an impact
Vulnerability	Lost sense of moral accountability
Risks	Demotion, sidelining, and termination
Communication Channels	Formal channels and expert opinions
Courage Needed	Candor within and outside of channels
Power to Influence	Formal assessments, briefings, and anonymous leaks

CHAPTER 10

THE ELITE CIRCLE

Influencers and the Power of Access

.

"To whom much is given, much will be required."
—LUKE 12:48

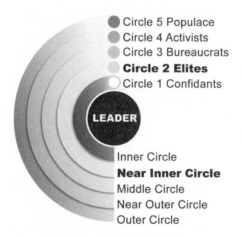

Who are the elite? Every society has them. They range from the wealthy to the tastemakers, from senior legislators and judicial officeholders to media pooh-bahs, past office-holders, and thought leaders in their field.

We use the term *elite* to include anyone who has the elevated stature to exert influence on the course of events more or less in line with the trajectory of the current power structure. By this definition, we draw a distinction between activists who may also have the power to influence the course of events but are typically doing so in ways that break with or seek to correct the existing power structure.

An elite may be the head of a national workers union or a global multinational corporation. They may be a civil servant who has risen to head an international financial institution, or their regulator. They may be the organizers of global events that attract the world's most effective influencers, or participants who are those influencers. Some are celebrity scientists or medical professionals who have gained access to A-list functions. Others are authors whose books have captured the imagination of millions of readers. They may be performers who sell out stadiums or philanthropists who have gained the world's approval for championing people in need. They may themselves be political figures who are seen as rising stars to be courted.

The common denominator is that they are perceived by those at the pinnacle of political leadership as having value to them or as posing potential competition or risk if not kept in the fold. Unlike most citizens, they are at one degree of separation from access to the highest political officeholders.

The existing social and economic systems work very well for elites, providing a highly privileged lifestyle worth vigorously defending and preserving. Depending on their role and the culture, this may be done with philosophic defenses of the system, large political contributions, high profile public endorsements, market manipulation, corruption that favors the political leader or even with private intelligence and paramilitary support.

All systems that favor an elite class contain the seeds of revolt by the underprivileged in that system. The underprivileged find or give rise to their own champions and political contenders. These can present or be perceived to present such a fundamental threat to the status quo that elites allow themselves to be driven into the arms of the prototyrant as their bulwark against loss of privilege.

It is natural enough for all parts of the polity to seek and protect their advantage. If not taken to extremes, this itself cannot be considered wrong except by those seduced by utopian visions despite their disappointing history.

Elites have an outsize stake in the functioning of the current system and use the levers of influence at their disposal. While the activist circle must work creatively to attract the attention of those in the highest circles, elites have easy access to the boardrooms, clubs, and media outlets that allow them to capture the notice of the political leader and their retinue in Circle 1, the leader's confidants. Though this is the case, as we shall see, it is highly dangerous for elites to become willing colluders and put their considerable resources behind the political figure who is already displaying the earmarks of a prototyrant.

THE DIVERSITY OF ELITES

Though I am differentiating elites from activists because they work within an existing system rather than seek to fundamentally change the system, this does not mean that elites all share a common interest or perspective. There are elites who can faithfully and effectively represent underserved and disempowered members of the populace to improve their circumstances within the system. They are elite because of their access to the inner circle and the central political officeholder.

Indeed, the most successful activists often become part of this elite circle when they gain the ability to open doors and create access to the inner circle. This can become a personal and political challenge, as other activists may then question their legitimacy. Nevertheless, they are an influential part of ever-changing political dynamics within a complex, heterogeneous system.

In the Civil Rights Movement in the United States in the 1960s, the Reverend Dr. Martin Luther King, Jr., found himself stretched between the roles of activist and elite. His large following—gained based on his fight for voting rights and an end to state-sanctioned apartheid and the nonviolent approach to which he was committed—found him straddling the roles of activist and elite insider. He achieved ample access to the US president and used it to forward the cause of justice.

This excerpt from a letter to Dr. King from then-US President Lyndon Johnson hints at this duality of outsider and insider roles. While Johnson was not a prototyrant, he was well known for his bullying behavior in getting others to fall in line. Here, he almost imperceptibly implies that as long as Dr. King can continue leading his people on a peaceful course of protest, he will have his support. King did this while younger, less patient activists chafed at what seemed his conciliatory style.

Dear Doctor King:
I fully appreciate the pressures and tensions under which you are laboring and I am confident you will continue to offer a course of leadership that will permit us to move toward our goal of universal suffrage.
Sincerely, Lyndon B. Johnson
Excerpt of letter of March 18th, 1965[1]

There is an ever-shifting balance of power as changes occur in the context of political leading and following. These changes are as varied as demography, migration, the rise and spread of religious beliefs, intellectual paradigms, power-altering communication technologies, economic arrangements, and so forth.

To perform the complex tasks of social and political governance, people organize themselves into many groups. Within this ecology a dynamic tension exists between the forces aiming to consolidate power and those advocating its distribution. A diversity of perspectives and interests contribute to rebalancing and realigning complex social systems. This is the necessary antidote to a trajectory of consolidation of political power into dictatorship or tyrannical rule.

While championing their own perspectives and interests, it is thus in the interest of elites to maintain the rights of other groups to operate within the political realm. There will be temptations to support the prototyrant's impulses to curtail the rights of groups on the other side of their issues and interests, but that would be a mistake. Such collusion would support a precedent that eventually could be turned on their own cherished rights. The most savvy and courageous elites will not only be wary of lending excessive support to a prototyrant but will also challenge those of their ilk who succumb to this temptation.

In April 1994, after years of racial struggle, the Republic of South Africa held its first inclusive national vote. The results were 252 seats in the National Assembly for the ANC under the leadership of Nelson Mandela, eighty-two seats for the National Party representing the white minority, forty-three seats for the Inkatha Freedom Party under Chief Buthelezi, which was the ANC's main political rival, with the remaining seats divided among smaller parties.

When the more belligerent ANC members voiced frustration that the ANC had not won all of the Black vote, Mandela sagely said this was a good thing, as now all had some voice in the political process.[2]

Yes, it is simpler if elites manipulate the political leader into silencing those who oppose their interests. But it is not safer. The consolidation of power by themselves and a prototyrant becomes a petri dish of corruption. The absence of competition breeds stagnation and calcification. A lack of legitimate paths to compete sends the divergent perspectives and energy underground, where they eventually explode in rebellion. Utilizing the privilege of elite access for retaining the distribution of power is in their long-term interest.

ELITES AS FOLLOWERS

Based on their life experience as "movers and shakers," elites are unlikely to conceive of themselves as followers. There may be marginal exceptions, such as very senior clergy who see themselves as followers of God or of God's representative on Earth. In parliamentary structures where there is a titular leader, they may understand their role as followers, even if they eschew the language.

More commonly, elites will view themselves as peers to the top political leaders, as they, too, are at the pinnacle of their profession or social class. Some may see themselves as kingmakers rather than as the king's subjects. There may be some truth to this perception.

Nevertheless, when we are speaking of the leader as the most senior authority in a structured political system, there is typically a factual power differential. Here, we can make use of the scholar Barbara Kellerman's definition of followers as individuals who have less formal power than the positional leader.[3] This may be true on a state or provincial level where the senior political executive has control over the policing and prosecution systems as well as local militia and the purse. It is certainly true on the national level where the sovereign, in the body of an individual executive, has command of the national intelligence agencies, federal police forces, all branches of the military, the mint, and the treasury. There is a significant "hard power" supremacy. The prototyrant, bent on control, may choose to turn these instruments against the interests of any particular elite or elite group that displeases them.

Therefore, it is in the elite's interest to move past an inflated sense of their agency and factor in the potential of the loss of power and status should they fall out of favor with a vengeful political leader. This is particularly true when an autocrat is consolidating power and on a trajectory to dictatorship and tyrannical rule.

If elites do not choose to distance themselves from or oppose the most senior political leader, they are by definition followers. How they show their support is critical. Do they offer it unquestioningly, align it with their values, give it superficially to get by, or maintain a stance that allows them to speak truth to power and challenge the autocrat's excesses?

ELITE PSYCHOLOGY

It is fatuous to claim a consistent psychology across all the individuals in a group or class. Yet, there can be a prevalent marker.

Individuals become elites in society through a range of pathways. Some are born into the existing power structure of class, ancestry, wealth, and racial privilege. Others come from a hardscrabble background and have worked or clawed their way to pinnacles in their field.

What most have in common is they now experience the

significant perks of privilege—the privilege of being taken seriously, of access to influential gatherings, future-shaping conversations, first-tier media outlets, private audiences, resources to fund favorite causes and A-list peers.

They stand in contrast to individuals who exhibit learned helplessness, sometimes found among less-fortunate segments of society. Experiments show that if you set someone up for failure, regardless of their efforts, they soon give up trying even when opportunities become available. Elites have learned that even if they don't at first succeed, there will always be additional pathways available to them. By the very fact of who they are and who they conceive themselves to be, they can work their will.

A personal sense of agency, balanced with communal responsibility, is a healthy attitude in life. Ideally, a culture would foster conditions that promote this attitude at every level of society. But any strength taken too far becomes a potential liability.

Elites can become sure, by the fact of their privilege, that they can manage, influence, or prevail in any situation. This results in ignoring or discounting warning signs that they may be wading into political waters with deadly undertows.

How does this become a problem?

THE PRIMARY ERROR

From a human rights perspective, there is no difference between a tyrant supposedly from the left or the right. Either will undermine the values of individual freedom and dignity as well as collective self-determination.

The primary error elites make is believing they can control the strongman they collude in creating. They fail to recognize that in creating the strongman, they tapped into the broad populace's urgent desire for a leader who will save them from the perceived deprivations and indignities of their lives. They fail to recognize that the populace views them, the elite, as the source of these deprivations. When the strongman has consolidated power, he can turn on the elites with reasonable confidence that the populace will support him and not them.

Mikhail Khodorkovsky benefited from the privatization of state industries after the fall of the Soviet Union. He became the richest of the oligarchs who acquired properties far below their actual value.

Resentment toward these oligarchs was widespread among the average Russian who was struggling to find their footing in the new and disorderly economy. Thus, when Khodorkovsky intimated there was corruption at the highest levels of government, Vladimir Putin, the prototyrant who was rapidly consolidating power and wealth, could manufacture legal charges against him, confiscate his business, and have him sentenced to fourteen years in jail. Putin only pardoned him after eight years in jail in exchange for promises to leave the country and not get involved in Russian politics.[4]

The message was brutal and clear: It does not matter who you are and how much you have. Now that I am the ultimate power in the land, do not thwart me in the slightest way.

Elites are playing with fire by elevating a would-be strongman who initially seems to support their privilege. It is true that their immediate self-interest may lie in countering a threat to their privilege from the supposed left. It may seem rational for them to support a populist leader from the supposed right.

This is a primary error, often a fatal one. If elites deem their self-interest is in elevating a particular strongman, they must, at the same time, institute checks on his power. The classic example we have seen of this is the time limit Roman senators placed on the individual with whom they invested dictatorial powers in a crisis. The US Congress has attempted something similar in putting time limits on the War Powers Resolution it has passed to allow the president the flexibility to respond to global events. Like the Roman senators, Congress has found it is not always as easy to withdraw this power as it was to confer it.

While it may be against their nature, a more viable strategy for elites to guard their privilege, rather than entrusting it to a prototyrant, might be to assess the excesses of their privilege and find ways to visibly reduce this while maintaining those elements most dear to them. This is a recipe for self-reform that is rarely found but would lessen the need to create a tyrant to counter populace-driven threats to their status.

It could be argued that as president of the United States, the wealthy Brahmin Franklin Delano Roosevelt applied this strategy despite the enmity it created within his elite class. Yet, with threats from the extreme left and right emerging in much of the world, history seems to show that his policies preserved his class and perhaps saved the world from the horror that international communism and vicious fascism both proved to be.

THE SECONDARY ERROR

Elites value the status and power they have inherited or earned. This is most often accompanied by ambition and competitiveness. Only a few escape this hubris.

Highly competitive elites may seize the opportunity to cooperate with the prototyrant's ambitions. They choose to enable the rise of the prototyrant as a tactical maneuver to gain favor and advantage over fellow elites. This tactic may provide short-term gain. They would do far better to consider long-term strategy.

Prototyrants know that if they can keep elites in a state of conflict with each other, those elites will have less attention and resources for questioning their moves to consolidate power. Elites should be savvy enough not to fall for this ploy. Yet, too often, they do.

To use an imperfect chess analogy—elites would be wise to keep their ultimate focus on the king rather than on knocking off his knights, bishops, and castles. The analogy, of course, needs expanding to focus as much on the moves and intentions of their own king as on the king of the adversary. Yet, it would still be an inadequate analogy, as the king on a chessboard must always follow the rules that limit their moves. A prototyrant who consolidates power no longer holds themselves bound by the rules and will turn on any of their allies as easily as on their adversary. If they need to knock off one of their pieces on the chessboard, there is nothing to stop them from doing so, as disorienting as this may be to the rest of the positions on the board.

When elites observe a fellow elite making a play to ingratiate themselves to the prototyrant at the expense of core values, it would be in their interest to pool their resources and interrupt this enabling behavior. Elites need each other. Compete, but do not seek to discredit and destroy. The collective strength of elites is a necessary informal balance to the prototyrant's weight of office. This was the driver of the nearly archetypical Magna Carta, which was created when fractious nobles coalesced to extract limits to the English king's power.

Most readers have learned that the Magna Carta was signed in the distant year of 1215. It is often presented as a foundational document on which increasingly democratic principles were built. While there is some truth to this, if you read its sixty-three clauses, you will find that most of them protect the rights of the nobility, including their right to limit interference by the Crown with the control of "the freemen" who were bound to their estates by custom and law. Clearly, this was more feudal than democratic.

Twenty-five barons signed the Magna Carta. Its relevance to this chapter is that the landed nobility, whom we would certainly include in the elite circle, wrested an agreement from the king to limit his power and pull them back from tyrannical excess. The baronial nobility historically warred with each other to protect or expand their lands and rights of succession. Nevertheless, it was clearly in their mutual interest to band together to interrupt the tyrannical use of sovereign power. While the document did not itself end the abuse of power, from that time forth, it provided a conceptual and nearly mythical, baseline for future struggles to limit royal prerogatives.

Elites would do well to hold its importance and power in mind as they find their balance of cooperation and competition with each other and the political leader. Alone and independent, the prototyrant can pick them off and remove them as roadblocks on his march to consolidate control. Together, operating in the window of opportunity, elites can check that consolidation and ensure power is sufficiently distributed to be curbed of its excesses.

CHAPTER 11

THE ELITE CIRCLE

Types of Elites and Their True Self-Interest

·

We have established that individuals can rise to elite status in a number of ways. In this chapter, we'll take a further look at the major types of elites and their particular power and vulnerability as they choose to follow or not.

WEALTHY ELITES

The most obvious type of elites that come to mind are the exceptionally wealthy. If they so choose, their wealth can provide them with leverage to support or oppose a political leader. Though they may choose to do neither, by their prominence, doing nothing is a passive form of support for the rising prototyrant.

Wealth may be used directly in the form of monetary contributions to campaigns, inaugural galas, support for public-private initiatives, or, in less transparent societies, for bankrolling the political leader's private life and assisting them in amassing clandestine illicit fortunes. This may include underwriting wars of choice, and thus, the gratuitous suffering caused becomes the shared moral responsibility of the financier.

This power buys the elite a certain amount of protection and safety. But taken too far, it increases their vulnerability. It is an oft-observed fact that when a sovereign becomes too financially indebted to a source of funds for their excessive appetites, it is easier to discredit and discharge the creditor than the debt.

It also becomes too easy for the prototyrant to tap the wealthy for support repeatedly—insinuating both advantage and safety to them—than to diversify raising revenue from a range of legitimate sources. Eventually, a tipping point is reached when the reluctant benefactor's resentment outweighs any advantage they see in cooperating. They then feel the sting of extortion and risk the prototyrant using the mechanisms of the State to question, scrutinize, cut them off from, or seize the assets that gave them whatever power they enjoyed.

The wealthy know they need to pony up considerable sums to "stay in the game," protect their interests, and accrue favor and influence. As in all things, there is too much of a good thing—especially a questionable thing. It may prove a more viable strategy to limit their support and diversify it among other individuals and groups who can serve as checks on the prototyrant's attempts to consolidate power. Risky? Yes. So is unfettered support for the political leader with tyrannical ambition.

The most courageous stance would be to recognize the signs of the petty tyrant who, with greater power, would become a full-blown tyrant and use their wealth early to derail that trajectory. If they fail, the tyrant will not soon forget. If they succeed, the world will never fully appreciate the harm avoided, as the prototyrant has not had the opportunity to show his full venom. Yet the wealthy should sleep better knowing they have done a service.

The word *follower* may not seem to apply to the wealthy, but the word *enabler* certainly would. Enabling is an act of supporting the dysfunction in a leader. This would be a form of following at its most dangerous.

POLITICAL ELITES

"Many mainstream politicians who preside over a democracy's collapse are not authoritarians committed to overthrowing the system; they are careerists who are simply trying to get ahead . . . Careerism is a normal part of politics. But when democracy is at stake, choosing political ambition over its defense can be lethal."
—STEVEN LEVITSKY AND DANIEL ZIBLATT,
authors of *The Tyranny of the Minority*

Political elites are in a class of their own. On the whole, they share a desire with the prototyrant to shape the governance of the country and place their mark on it. As political creatures, they weigh the various power centers and make decisions about aligning with or competing with them. It is not that they are without principles or a desire to serve; rather, they never lose sight of the chessboard on which they are playing and which moves will prove strategic.

This presents a dangerous potential for colluding with the prototyrant. He is ascending in office. He can reward or punish, include or exclude, make or break. Or so it seems.

The political elite share in the primary and secondary errors we have discussed—they intuitively understand the principle enunciated by the German political theorist Carl Schmitt that politics is about friend and foe. There is a need to align, or seem to align, with one or another side. Failing to do this invites the Texas pejorative that the only thing you find in the middle of the road are dead armadillos.

Yet alignment with the prototyrant carries its risks. As they edge closer to the line from autocrat to dictator or tyrant, those closely identified with them will carry the stain into their future. It is strategically safer, though morally questionable, to thread the needle of being sufficiently sup-portive of the prototyrant to avoid being targeted by them, while putting enough daylight between themselves and the prototyrant to claim they have been a moderating influence.

Look at how much energy is spent on figuring out how to survive and remain relevant, which could be spent in ser-vice to the betterment of life in the polity! Yet, the real world of politics seems to require this. Except when one makes a different choice. There are political elites who, for some combination of principal and strategic differentiation, will carve a path in clear distinction to the prototyrant or even in opposition to them. This, too, requires considerable skill and energy, yet contains the potential to lead their peers away from the ultimately self-destructive course of colluding with the prototyrant's attempts to consolidate power.

Spain has played an interesting role in relation to tyrants and prototyrants in the last century. Growing up, my educated and politically conscious relatives refused to travel to Spain while the fascist dictator Francisco Franco ruled the country from 1939 to 1979, a discouraging forty-year reign.

Following his death, Spain restored its democracy under a constitutional monarch. The transition was marred by economic crisis and separatist terrorism—potentially fertile grounds for another autocratic leader with dictatorial ambition.

In 1981, in the midst of Spain's election of a new prime minister, civil guardsmen stormed the building in which the parliament held its session, guns drawn, with the intent of installing their own conservative general as prime minister. The constitutional monarch, King Juan Carlos, intervened to support the democratic process. But it was questionable if his intercession would have been sufficient had not political leaders across the ideological spectrum also vocally and forcefully denounced the coup.

In support of these elite followers standing up for democracy, more than a million citizens marched in the streets. All factions of the political landscape recognized a

continued

TO STOP A TYRANT

mutual interest in preserving their still-fragile democracy. The coup leaders—a clique of prototyrants—were arrested, tried, and given significant prison terms, ending the specter of further coups.[1]

When I went to Spain a decade or so later, it was as a consultant to the Club de Madrid, a world-class organization that was committed to the development of new and emerging democracies. I was able to do this consultant work in Spain because courageous followers had thwarted the emergence of a would-be tyrant at the right time and in the right way.

A complicating factor for political elites is whether they are from the same party or faction as the autocratic leader, or in opposition. In opposition, they have, to some degree, the safety of numbers of their partisans and great incentive to disrupt the advancement of a prototyrant. It is members of the autocrat's own party or faction that face the largest dilemma. Political norms dictate that they give loyal support to their leader. These are enforced in a multitude of painful, informal, and formal ways. Yet, it is responsible members of the leader's party who are best positioned to check the impulses of the prototyrant. Courage, political savvy, and persuasive communication are all needed to play this crucial role.

The most gifted of these political elites will create their own coterie to help shape the narrative so they cannot be defined as malcontents or traitors by the prototyrant's camp. While they are engaged in these necessary preemptive and flanking moves, they will not lose sight of the prosocial goals for which they desire political power.

How is followership expressed in this game of three-dimensional chess? First, their followership in relation to the prototyrant is highly conditional. It will be given when the autocrat is willing to make moves that benefit the body politic. It will be withdrawn from all moves that seek to weaken the institutions that exist to place healthy checks on the use of unitary power.

Followership is also expressed in the political elite's circles. They, too, have five circles of followers around them. These must be treated with the respect and regard they do not enjoy from the prototyrant. It is the followers in those circles who will ultimately enable the political elite to be successful or not.

These savvy political elites do not impose the requirements of unquestioning conformity and obedience on their circles of followers. Discipline, yes. But not yes-manship. This diversity and authenticity of inputs is their soft power advantage over the prototyrant. While they are buffering the prototyrant's impulses to consolidate and abuse power, their courageous followers are making sure they don't get infected with the same disease. They are receiving a range of perspectives that are not available to the prototyrant, who is in an information bubble, made impervious by the demand for obsequiousness. Their strategy can be based on the realities of changing popular needs and sentiments, while the prototyrant is increasingly out of touch.

Yet, there is a caveat. Their followers—constituents and

prospective voters—may have become infected with the prototyrant's vitriol and be placing great pressure on their representatives to fall in line. It is here that the dual role of the elected representative comes into play—they, too, are both leaders and followers. To stay elected, they must remain aligned with the broad sentiments of their constituency. To fulfill their oath of office, they must educate their constituency on what they are learning from their insider vantage point. Courage is required when this creates distance from their activist followers. This is the eternal dance of responsible democracy—knowing when to follow and when to lead.

MEDIA ELITES

Just as there are all levels of politics, from the hometown mayor to the presidential palace, there are media outlets, from the hometown weekly to the prime-time broadcaster, major newspaper publisher, and influential social media pundit. The larger the number of eyeballs or eardrums reached, the greater the potential for influence. These are the media elite.

While straight news reporting may seem to be a nonpolitical act, that is an illusion. Any discretion about which stories to cover and how prominently to cover them has a political dimension and impact. Even the absence of a story is a political act when the prototyrant or their detractors are counting on its coverage.

If a media platform or personality is on the political fringes, they may fit in better with the activist circle of followers. Their peripheral position allows them to cover stories with more directness and less concern about language that may be considered disloyal or inflammatory by the prototyrant. They may be shut down, or worse, but their moral position remains untarnished if their reporting is based on the best available data.

It is somewhat different with media in the elite circle. We are defining the *elite* by their ability to access the leader and his inner circle. Earning and maintaining this status requires its own dance. They must be compelling enough to acquire and hold a large audience while being sufficiently conforming to keep a seat at the table. If they are seen as sidestepping sensitive issues by their audience, they lose credibility. If they are seen by the political leadership as too confrontational, they may find their access diminished, or in a rapidly advancing tyranny, their media platforms blocked. Their self-interest and public duty appear to require walking a line between these poles. Access is their currency. When does this dance become collusion by providing a patina of legitimacy for a regime that increasingly violates appropriate boundaries?

As we have seen, there is a legitimate need for sufficient power to enact a regime's pledges to the populace. Where that point is may not be a science. All regimes seek to garner power for themselves. However, cumulative acts of consolidating power are a barometer reading that warns of approaching storms. The media may pay insufficient attention to the signs. The news organizations to which they belong typically lean in one political direction or another. If they generally support the political party and leader, questioning their accrual of power may be implicitly discouraged. If their news organization leans to the opposite pole, they may be too quick to condemn power politics that are being played within cultural norms. Serious media may show support for the prosocial acts of an otherwise autocratic regime without betraying their responsibility to report on behavior that is dangerous to the polity.

At times, however, it is easier to focus on the salacious, which attracts viewership while avoiding the displeasure of the prototyrant or of their own audience. Petty scandals and manufactured conflicts become a drug of choice, though these are a sideshow and distraction from the progression of autocracy to tyranny. Because prototyrants are charismatic, and because as populists they tend to excite audiences by smashing through customary norms of behavior, the elite media are often torn between how much play to give these antics and how much to ignore them and limit their oxygen supply.

It is an error to give outsized attention to distractions that allow the consolidation of power to become obscured. The media plays a necessary role in a system where they are an element in the balance of power. Their focus should be on the main event: the capacity of society to remain relatively just, free, and responsive to the populace's needs

If the autocratic trend of the regime warrants calling out, elite media will need to weigh the value of access or even personal safety against the responsibility to employ their megaphone to do so. It is their great responsibility to attract and focus attention rather than add to the cacophony of swirling information, disinformation, diversions, and deflections. They, too, will need to courageously balance their leader and follower roles in relation to their audience, as well as to the political regime.

In the chapter on coalitions, we will see a particularly poignant example of this during the 1970s Watergate scandal, when a courageous press risked both political and legal sanction for pursuing a story of great adverse consequence to the administration of US President Richard Nixon.

INTERMEDIARY ELITES

As this book goes through its final editing stages, I am called to violate the stance I took in Chapter 6 on activist followers, which was to refrain from wading into the ever-changing waters of technology and social media tools that augment or constrain the trajectory of autocrats to political tyranny. They morph too rapidly to weather well on the dried ink of a printed book. I take this risk after listening to an interview with Seth Lazar on "Political Philosophy in the Age of AI" and recommend his thinking to the reader.[2]

I will not attempt to summarize Lazar's incisive observations and ways of approaching the opportunities and risks posed by artificial intelligence as applied to social relations. Instead, I will use his terminology to identify an additional type of elite whose specialized power can be harnessed in support of, or to brake, the accumulation of political power by a prototyrant.

Intermediary elites are the large companies or autocratic government propaganda apparatuses that create and manage the algorithms determining what information may be posted, boosted, replicated, scrubbed, or monetized. They are not technically a subset of media elites as they are not creating content but rather are enabling or disabling content and the information, ideas, and calls to action these carry. Potentially, they can be of great help to a prototyrant or pose a significant threat.

In addition to any social benefits they may perform, these platforms have the capacity to magnify concepts and images that distort the public space and weaken the ability of heterogeneous societies to maintain a sense of coherent identity. Hate speech, racial bias, conspiracy theories, and falsified images propagated by unwitting site managers, meme promoters, or clandestine surrogates create confusion, alarm, and social fragmentation that can play into a prototyrant's disruptive tactics. Fomenting a sense of chaos creates justification for their savior message.

In response to these corrosive elements, we have seen the beginning of regulatory and self-directed initiatives to curtail the worst outcomes of politically subversive operatives, including the bias that can be embedded in large language models used by artificial intelligence. Those elites who own, plan for, and manage technology behemoths, as well as scrappy innovators, will need to act with increased responsibility for the consequences of new technologies they bring online. They will always be quicker and more agile at finding solutions that balance free expression and society's need for reliable information. Public/private watchdogs are also positioned to identify and call out needed change while bureaucratic regulators and higher courts play catch-up.

The autocrat who is beginning to demonstrate pro-totyrannical impulses to control information, and mute criticism, is drawn to these elites who provide intermediary platforms from which to reach the populace. Depending on where they are on the trajectory to consolidating power, they will first rely on the promise of rewards for their support and, later on, the threat of penalties for their lack of submissive cooperation.

The promise of financial gain for early support of the autocratic regime will be difficult to resist. Yet, the prospect for gain needs to be weighed against the risks of enabling the prototyrant, including damage to the platform's brand and defections in protest of its collusion. While power is still sufficiently distributed, the platforms will and should come under pressure from activists and the bureaucracy to curb practices that patently undermine trusted political space. It is reasonable for the society they serve to hold them accountable for the consequences of their policies.

Beyond these external constraints, the strain intermediaries experience serving two masters—a populace who deserves objectively good information and a prototyrant who defines *good* in terms of their power-driven agenda— will make for miserable conditions in which to enjoy their elite status. As intermediaries, they are in the middle of roiling and consequential political dynamics. They will need to bring their political skills to navigate these churning waters. Forming coalitions with other elite intermediaries to do more right than wrong will serve as a counterweight to a prototyrant's increasing monopolization and abuse of power. But only if not left too late.

CULTURAL STARDOM

All cultures produce stars. They are the awesomely talented or the idealized representations of our cultural fantasies. Assisted by coteries of publicity agents and social media wunderkind, they work their way into our collective consciousness and become household names recognizable in daily conversation.

For most of these one-in-a-million personages, it is in their personal and professional interest to remain political eunuchs, threatening no one in the inner circles of governance. There are several problems with this.

The first is the truism that remaining silent in the face of an increasingly oppressive regime implicitly aids the regime. The second is that their fame makes them targets for the regime to woo as bling to their necklaces of fabricated legitimacy. They are invited to the presidential palace to serenade the autocrat and two hundred other elites who are similarly kept in the fold by the bragging rights of closeness to power. Where rich performance fees are offered, these sweeten the opportunity and compound the questionable morality of the invitation.

It is tempting to rationalize accepting the invitation and riding the wave as an in-group player at this moment in history. But once aboard, how do you refuse a seat on the presidential plane or refuse to be photographed at the gala, embracing the smiling prototyrant and his family? You did not intend to be a visibly supportive follower, but you have been played into posing as one.

"Jennifer Lopez is feeling the heat this week for singing 'Happy Birthday' to the authoritarian ruler of Turkmenistan. The former Soviet state is considered 'one of the world's most repressive countries'; it once shut down the entire Internet in order to stop a video of its president falling off a horse from disseminating.

"Nor is J.Lo the first pop star to sing before googling, unwittingly bringing international human rights abuses to the attention of the *Us Weekly* crowd. From Sting to 50 Cent, the music industry's free speech beneficiaries are the preferred American and British export of cash-flush dictators everywhere."[3]

Now, *your* followers have a dilemma. Those who are leery of the prototyrant's more obvious moves to curtail freedoms and dissension must decide whether to keep supporting you or mount a secondary boycott against your artistic output. You have quickly gained something and lost something. Do you backpedal or double down? Either move has its consequences.

How might you have avoided this perilous crossroads? First, have your team do its due diligence and avoid the temptation of outsized performance fees or novel publicity.

The Beatles seem to have done this when they toured the Philippines during the dictatorial reign of Ferdinand Marcos. Their manager maintained a policy of not accepting invitations to embassies or official functions, which made declining problematic invitations somewhat easier. Imelda Marcos, the dictator's politically adroit wife, exerted significant pressure on the group, including closing the airport so they couldn't leave the country. By holding their ground and refusing to be trotted out as guests at this command performance, they escaped the outcome of a photograph with the dictatorial couple.

There may also be an unconscious factor at work here. Just as your fans have become somewhat dazzled by your fame, you may become dazzled by the rarefied atmosphere at the peak of the governance mountain. Paradoxically, the allure of fame and influence that you cultivate in the world of celebrity must be resisted on the stage of political power that is being amassed without regard to human rights and dignity.

You may first do this quietly in your noticeable absence from high-profile events. Soon, you recognize that a point of no return is approaching, calling you to distance yourself from the abuses of power publicly. Your star that has risen now requires you to use its brilliance to shine a light on the emerging peril. Those in the wide footprint of your celebrity may be brought to recognize the dangers of being indifferent to the trajectory of the prototyrant or of following them. In a nearly mystical sense, you are pitting your charisma against theirs, which is seducing the populace.

But remember the window for doing this is *before* they consolidate power. Afterward, even your widely recognized voice is likely to be insufficient against the vast enforcement machinery at the tyrant's disposal, and you become a target for silencing.

Those of us who are not political or cultural elites can, at times, be awed when we encounter a star in their field. When I saw the actor Richard Gere in one of the US House of Representatives office buildings, I needed to restrain myself from acting on the rush of recognition and excitement I felt. When I was at an inaugural ball for a newly sworn-in president of the United States, my wife nearly broke through a barrier rope when she saw the musician Paul Simon only feet away. Celebrities have to learn to live with this reaction their presence generates in others.

Ironically, we can also see film, music, and sports celebrities experience a similar response when they come into the presence of a political figure who has attained star status. I had the privilege of facilitating retreats for the prominent civil rights leader John Lewis and his congressional office staff. The walls in his office were decorated floor to ceiling with photos of people from all walks of life meeting with this legendary figure. It amused me when I read of an entertainment celebrity who spoke about their meeting with John Lewis or another of their political heroes. They, too, sounded like starstruck fans—better they pick a John Lewis for their adulation than a charismatic autocrat who would be all too happy to be photographed with them.

THE JUDICIARY

In some respects, the judiciary should not be classified as followers. By design and intention, their very essence is to exist and act independently of the executive function of government. They are their own authority, following only the law and their impartial interpretation of its application to cases.

Of course, this is the theory. In every system of governance, the way judges are selected or raised to positions of prominence implicitly creates a potential bias for or in contrast to the executive. To carry out their sworn oath of office, judges will need the strength of character to perform their duties fairly, regardless of pressure to issue rulings that favor the power-seeking autocrat. In this respect, they must be the most faithful followers of all—followers of the law and the principles of justice on which it should rest. These will not always be the same. In the twentieth century, judges were faced with abhorrent racist laws in Nazi Germany, in apartheid South Africa, and in the segregation era of the United States.

In countries in which an autocrat is beginning to consolidate power ruthlessly, judges may become the most serious impediment of all and, therefore, the target of extralegal pressure to back down. The best will find the courage to perform their sacred duty of upholding the morality on which the law should rest and will do so within the limits and discretion of their role.

When we talk about "brakes" on the prototyrant's juggernaut, the judiciary has a critical role to play. It typically has no hard power to enforce its findings. Rather, it relies on its moral authority with the populace to require compliance from the executive branch. Therefore, it must carefully guard and continue to earn its moral standing.

The number of judges relative to the size of a government's administrative branches is minuscule. However, the judicial system includes other sworn officers of the court, including all those certified to practice law. This group of elites must also view themselves as a bulwark against the excessive, and certainly extraconstitutional accrual of power by a proto-tyrant. Revisiting once again the contemporary event of the Israeli prime minister seeking to weaken the independence of the judiciary, hundreds of Israeli lawyers marched in the streets to protest this attempted incursion on judicial power.

In normal political times, the elite of the judicial system enjoy the privileges and perks of their position. When the political freedom of the nation is at risk, it is time for these elites to rise to their role as protectors of the balance of power and its just use.

RELIGIOUS ELITES

In some societies, there is no distinction between religious elites and political elites. In others, there is a strong wall between them. Either way, they tend to have direct access to huge swaths of the populace and influence with them. This is an irresistible target for the prototyrant to court or nullify.

In many cases, the shrewd prototyrant will pose as befriending the major religious sect, or at least dissemble that they mean it no harm. It is extremely enticing for the leaders of these sects to give the prototyrant public support, or at least studiously refrain from criticizing their regime.

There is apparently much to be gained, or at least much less to lose, in terms of their temporal power and ability to continue serving their faithful.

It is supremely ironic to ask religious leaders, "What price their soul?" Yet this is the question they must ask themselves if they choose to conform or, worse, collude with the prototyrant. Power is power, whether in military uniform, judicial robes, or clerical garb. It is hard to risk losing it. But that very power carries with it the burden of deploying it in service of the good.

Your congregants—your followers—constitute a decisive segment of the populace, the ultimate source of political power. If you signal your support for the prototyrant, you are enabling and paving the trajectory to full tyranny. Your minimum obligation is not to lend the prestige of your role to support an illusion of the prototyrant as a defender of the faith or messianic messenger. Nor should you use this illusion as the rationale for your own choices.

Beyond that, your role becomes more delicate. There is a legitimate argument for keeping the political out of the worship service. All those present deserve to be held in the embrace of the faith. Inevitably, political views will range across the spectrum. Using the pulpit to cajole for or against the prototyrant violates the sanctity of the worship space. If doing so becomes a drumbeat, you will literally be preaching to the choir, as those who do not share your views will withdraw or find congregations better aligned with their politics.

Some will argue that this stand is a dereliction of moral duty. In the face of a widespread campaign against vulnerable minorities, doesn't the spiritual leader have a duty to speak for the voiceless? To uphold the sanctity of all human life? This is a powerful argument.

An answer to the conflicting obligations lies in using the power of the pulpit to speak against specific immoral policies without targeting the regime itself. This may be thought to split hairs, but that is the very point. One can remain a follower of the duly constituted political regime while vocally questioning egregious policies. This is the very essence of courageous followership.

To those who do not bear responsibility for a congregation, this may seem too weak a response to the increasingly abusive use of power. Yet it may be the appropriate response for a vested religious leader—still an act of courage and, in the best case, a corrective to the autocrat who learns the limits of their "free pass" for accruing and abusing governing power.

Should the prototyrant fail to absorb the lessons being taught to the populace from the pulpit and continue on an egregious path toward tyrannical rule, the religious elite can follow their source of moral guidance and choose to become activists. This is the measured, latent power of elite privilege. The challenge is timing: too soon, you lose the congregation; too late, you lose the window of opportunity. Indeed, it is a time for guidance, judgment, and courage.

INTEREST GROUP LEADERS

Collections of people in organized interest groups are the fabric of political life.

Once governments become the source of laws, rules,

defense and public order, social welfare programs, taxation that funds these, and the budget to implement them, interest groups will naturally coalesce around mutual perceived interests. They will seek to influence the various branches of government to support and favor their competing agendas.

Industry roundtables, small business associations, national ethnic advocacy coalitions, geographic and demographic interest groups, workers' unions, educational associations, and so forth, all develop effective government relations arms. Those who rise to become the heads of the largest of these interest groups enter the circle of elites. By the political power they represent, they have earned access, and often a seat, at the table. Once these are gained, they can also be lost. This weighs heavily on how the interest group elites relate to the emerging prototyrant and their regime.

If these elites have done their work well, the interest group has effectively told their story to all levels and points of the government whose support helps their cause. They have used communication strategies to create a worthy image in the minds of the broad populace. By these accomplishments, they reduce their existential reliance on the emerging prototyrant, as their interests will be defended at many points of the system.

Yet, the temptation to curry favor with the rising autocrat is strong. Their interest group's cause can be boosted or made more complicated with a few words from the autocrat's office, particularly those who are vindictive about breaches of support. It is here that the long game needs to be assessed, planned for, and sold to the interest group members. It is vital that interest group elites maintain the trust of their members and allies so they have the latitude to act on long-term benefits at the expense of short-term disfavor.

The closer the interest group is to the nationalist agenda of the prototyrant, the more challenging this becomes. The low-hanging fruit made available by the autocrat's agenda is tempting, and the serpents in the garden will make it sound worth any long-term potential consequence. Yet, it is the fiduciary responsibility of the interest group elite that must provide the center of gravity for their decision-making. A genuine passion for the group's cause and care for its repute need to be drawn on to face down the autocrat and the chorus of those tempted by his enticements.

Counterintuitively, if the autocrat and his inner circle know they can unquestionably count on the group's support, it will receive less attention than comparable groups the autocrat needs to court. This provides the elite interest group with room to send signals to not take them for granted. If those signals are heeded, the interest group has an opportunity to make requests on behalf of their coalition. These can include measures that restrain the consolidation of the autocrat's power. The greater the influence an interest group enjoys, the greater the responsibility to act as a brake on that trajectory.

Interest group leaders may not deem they have the political space to break with or oppose the autocratic ruler. Yet, their political savvy, which elevated them to the highest levels of the interest group, can be employed to navigate the relationship with the autocrat and minimize enabling their prototyrannical tendencies. When they see an opening to act courageously, they are ready.

Viktor Orbán and the Trade Unions

As of this writing, Viktor Orbán is the prime minister of Hungary. His career path is of interest to us as it is almost a model of a worrisome progression toward tyrannical rule while not fully there.

He began his political career in the fateful year of 1989, just before the fall of the Soviet Union. He played a leadership role in the student movement in support of democratic reforms, calling for the removal of Soviet troops from Hungary and a new democratic constitution—a promising start for a potential reformer.

The following year, he was elected to the National Assembly and worked his way into the prime minister position in 1998. He is credited with a number of positive developments, including the invitation to join NATO. In 2002, he became the leader of the opposition, a peaceful and orderly transition of power.

A skillful politician, Orbán regained the prime minister's office in 2010 and now, in 2024, is its longest-serving incumbent—but not without disturbing signs.

In 2013, he became another political leader who pushed through amendments to the constitution that reduced judicial oversight of executive action. For the last decade, his increasingly autocratic behavior has been a thorn in the side of both NATO and the European Union, of which Hungary is a member.

On our trajectory, he is on the edge of the window, bordering on dictatorial use of power. Some will argue he is fully there. Yet, there has still been room for pushback. When his government went a step too far in angering the working class in 2018, the worker's union movement was able to get thousands of citizens into the streets to oppose the objectionable policies. A "pocketbook issue" such as that one tends to open space for more fundamental criticism of the increasingly autocratic regime.

The outcome? Not much changed, which is often the reality of even well-led popular protests. Given Hungary's long memory of brutal crackdowns by the Soviet Union (the context of this leader-follower relationship), using armed force was not an option for an Hungarian leader. However, the unions did put the regime on notice that there are limits to how it wields power. At times, interest group opposition combined with international reactions may be sufficient to interrupt the potential progression to a full-blown tyrant.[4]

OTHER ELITES

There are other paths to elite status in which one has access to the inner governing circle and even to the leader at the top of the pyramid. They are as novel as individual human beings.

In a pandemic, well-placed public health officials find themselves with access to the highest levels. In wartime, former military flag officers may be called on for perspective and advice. Doors open for those who can raise large amounts of money to fund a political campaign or a cherished program.

A hero of a national tragedy or victory may find themselves with unexpected platforms on which to express their views and political preferences.

If one has gained the status to command the attention of the prototyrant or their inner circle, the question must be asked: How can I best use this access to create positive change?

The most effective means is usually to stick close to one's expertise or role. In a country devoted to the automobile, this is often referred to as "staying within your lane." In this lane, you have credentials. You command attention, your thoughts on policies best suited to a situation are given consideration. As a prototyrant's initiatives further or impede legitimately formulated policy, you can make a case for supporting beneficial actions or for opposing those that harm the people and principles being badly served by that policy.

Elites are performing a high-wire act. If they gain a spotlight, the rising political leader sees them as an asset. If they gain too much public approval, an ambitious politician sees them as a competitor for the public's attention and a potential threat. Most who rise to elite status have an inner gyroscope to help them balance on this high wire. Where they most often go wrong is to see themselves as too important to dismiss or sideline. A degree of objectivity about the limits of their power needs to be programmed into the gyroscope by their followers.

Equally, they can go wrong by closing their eyes to how they are enabling power grabbing by the prototyrant. We can all be guilty of rationalizing our self-interested actions that conflict with vaguely defined ethical boundaries. Elites who do this exert leverage that causes more damage than most of those in less-elevated circles. It is their responsibility to ask themselves more rigorous questions about when to follow this leader, when to cease following, and when to oppose. As always, the window for making these determinations does not remain open indefinitely.

ELITES	SUMMARY
Available Information	Confidential briefings, market maker insights
Incentives to Follow	Expectation of influence, retaining access and privileges
Vulnerability	Belief they can control the prototyrant
Risks	Loss of own power base or access to and support from the autocrat
Communication Channels	Private communiqués and audiences, access to top-tier media
Courage Needed	Taking displeasing positions
Power to Influence	Deep pocket financing, control of institutions that can support or oppose

CHAPTER 12

THE CONFIDANT

CIRCLE

Who Are They Really?

.

"No matter how noble your goals or how strong your
morals are, the pressures and pleasures of power impact
every one of us. A protection and antidote for this is paying
great attention to who we gather around us. "
—RUTH TURNER, senior advisor to former
UK prime minister Tony Blair

THE INNER CIRCLE

The inner circle of followers—Circle 1—has extraordinary
access to the political leader. They may have "walk-in" rights
to their office, with or without scheduled appointments.

They have the leader's personal communication information. They may be a childhood friend or a lifelong legal advisor; they may dine with them in their quarters, celebrate birthdays, or even be the one whose head lies on the pillow next to theirs at night.

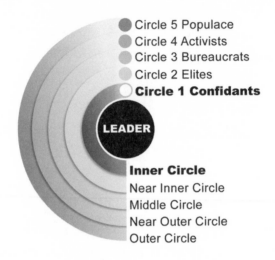

- Circle 5 Populace
- Circle 4 Activists
- Circle 3 Bureaucrats
- Circle 2 Elites
- **Circle 1 Confidants**

LEADER

Inner Circle
Near Inner Circle
Middle Circle
Near Outer Circle
Outer Circle

These intimate confidants see the person behind the role and its public face. They see the leader when they are tired, sick, unsure of themselves, or too sure of themselves. Because of the inordinate access and close-up perceptions, they, in particular, are responsible for detecting the rise of destructive tendencies in the leader and making choices that can interrupt the trajectory toward a failed incumbency or tyrannical reign. There is a gravitational pull in this circle to be colluders. If they can resist that pull and act as courageous followers, they do themselves, the leader, and the polity the highest service.

COMPOSITION OF THE INNER CIRCLE

While democracies may have means of excluding proposed appointments to the second circle—heads of agencies and ministries—they rarely, if ever, have formal mechanisms for vetting those in the leader's intimate first circle.

Yet, it is these closest followers who will be with the leader in the existential windows where the leader is tempted to consolidate power and step firmly on the road to a tyrannical regime. Who they are and what they do at those moments can be pivotal.

The confidants with whom leaders most closely surround themselves are indicators of the likely trend of their use or abuse of power. In societies where people choose their leaders through various democratic processes, citizens engaged in the selection need to be as interested in the leader's political inner circle as they are in the leader. And so must the media.

As inner circle conversations and agreements are often carefully guarded secrets, it becomes the role of investigative media to identify who the leader is surrounding themselves with and if there are any truly dangerous actors in that circle. Just as crucially, actors in the first circle who are aware of the pernicious tendencies of another actor in that circle need to collectively create constraints on that actor or advocate for their exclusion.

Another complicating paradox is also operative. The leader requires strong followers around them who can support their capacity for using power and also restrain the misuse of that power. It is no easy task to discern how this balance plays out in these individuals. None are angels. All, to some degree, practice the art of masking the worst facets of themselves.

In a perfect world, this group of egotistical individuals would be served by counselors and facilitators who bring out their virtues and help minimize characteristics that abuse power. Perfect worlds don't exist. The best we may be able to do is describe the attributes of ideal behavior and seek to form a culture that values them. This will involve the various societal institutions for culture formation and intergenerational transmission.

Meanwhile, the best of these confidants must step back and look at the leader's tenure from the perspective of their legitimate term or, where none exists, their likely term and how to conclude it with three things in mind:

- Achievement of whatever prosocial mark the leader is committed to and capable of effecting.

- Leaving the office with those achievements and their reputation well regarded and unmarred by abuse of power.

- Safety for the leader, themselves, and their families, by retaining different forms of legitimate power that protect them during and after leaving office.

TYPES OF CONFIDANTS

The prototyrant surrounds himself with a few key types of followers in his inner circle.

The Young

A surprising type of confidant is young or marginalized. Perhaps they started in a minor role—driver, valet, caddy— and caught the eye of the leader for their dedication to his needs. In one way or another, fate has brought them together, and they now occupy positions with the leader that are far beyond what their resumes qualify them for. Not having vast experience with life, they are prone to seeing the leader as a hero, towering above others, feeding their outsized ego.

A young friend who had worked in the office of the vice president of the United States was asked what she missed most about the time she was in that position. You might think it would be the chance to make a difference in the world. Without missing a beat, she said, "The plane!" There was nothing like being driven right to Air Force Two on the tarmac, missing all the airport lines, and feeling so special when she boarded with the VP.

The seasoned professionals who are trying to serve, control, or manipulate the leader are resentful of the seemingly unearned access or influence these youthful devotees enjoy. This follower may not be particularly well qualified but earns their place by their unswerving loyalty. Or, they may have special skills, typically related to their generation, that are valued by the leader when used in strict service to their agenda.

This type of inner circle follower does not have a power base, so they pose little potential threat to the leader. By having this plum position, they "owe him everything." These followers, inflated with a sense of power and purpose and lacking the perspective that comes with experience, often become the most fanatical in enforcing the leader's dominance. They can be the most dangerous colluders and least likely to check prototyrannical behavior; that is unless they can tune in to an inner voice of those who raised them with strong values of fairness and kindness—values that are noticeably absent in the leader they are serving. When that inner voice can no longer be stilled, they may be able to extricate themselves and find ways to tell what they saw in the inner circle.

The Powerful

A contrasting type of follower that the prototyrant selects for their inner circle, or just outside it, are well-established individuals—business moguls, former military officers, political rivals they bested—to provide a patina of legitimacy. These may have egos, ambitions, and power bases as large as the leader's. It is a risk bringing them this close, but it is considered a necessary one while the leader is consolidating their power. This is a marriage of convenience.

Because of their status, there is an opportunity to modulate the leader's behavior if they see that doing so is in their own interest. They have the experience and the stature and carry the implicit threat of their base of support. While they have this capacity, they may choose not to risk affronting the leader until it is too late and the leader no longer needs them.

A danger is their susceptibility to using their position to

win favor for the special projects of their powerful friends. Gifts may be offered to them for this service, which they rationalize as unproblematic, while to the rest of the world, they are clearly bribes, regardless if they don't technically trip ethics wires. When their integrity is compromised, they find it harder to call the leader to task for his ethical compromises or even to see them.

There are impressive exceptions to this. While working with the US Congress, we would host visiting legislators from emerging democracies. Our mandate was to expose them to the various institutional mechanisms that allow Congress to match the resources of the executive branch and thus serve as a check on its power. The visiting legislators could then consider these for creating a better balance of power in their governments.

We designed program agendas rich with exposure both to members of Congress and to congressional staff and support units. If we called on particularly interesting figures too often, we were authorized to pay them a small honorarium, within congressional rules and with full tax reporting.

One of these was a close aide to the speaker of the house. At a later point, we were seeking funding for the work we did for congressional offices and approached this senior staff member for his assistance. His immediate response was, "Didn't you pay me an honorarium for speaking to visiting legislators? I need to return that to you before I do any favors that could be interpreted as payback for the money I received."

This level of fiscal probity served him well for the rest of his impressive career.

The Family

The third category is family and near family, early childhood friends, and the families of marriage partners. In most cultures, "blood is thicker than water," and family loyalty is the highest level of loyalty. These are the most trusted confidants; at times, they are the only ones fully trusted by the leader. This is so if they are not political liabilities or jealous competitors. Those will be kept out of view as much as possible, and their pronouncements and behavior will be monitored and protected against.

Trusted family members often hold no formal role in the administration but are understood to have outsize power and not to be crossed. They are cultivated by followers from other circles as conduits to the leader, sometimes with hidden economic incentives that will be problematic for the leader when they come to light.

I have worked with scores of congressional offices. In every one of them, the chief of staff knew not to get on the wrong side of the spouse of the member of Congress. At the same time, it was helpful if the spouse knew their favor was being curried by an endless queue of people wanting to influence the legislative agenda. They particularly need political antennae to detect radioactive situations from which to insulate their partner. However, if the spouse has as much or more political ambition than the formal political leader, their outsized influence can wreak havoc. In this case, it is the staff who will need to discreetly provide the elected leader protection.

It is possible that one or more of these trusted family

members may have the conscience, savvy, and stature to modulate worsening autocratic behavior. If they can do so, they are acting in the true long-range interests of the leader and the family. Other confidants and elites who are concerned about the political leader's growing consolidation of power would do well to protect a family counterweight from being undermined by those benefiting from that consolidation.

THE COMMON VANTAGE POINT

What is common to each of these confidants is that they see the "real soul" of the leader—not the manufactured, packaged, heroic cutout.

Given this perspective (not filtered through a public relations lens), the inner circle is better positioned to distinguish between a skilled persuader who is capable of productive and beneficial leadership and those more likely to use power for personal and destructive ends. The would-be leader cannot ascend to power without the support of confidants amplifying their message and watching their back. They are critical assets to the leader. If they ignore the unvarnished dark side of the leader, they can also become enablers of tyrannical impulses. If they resist willful blindness, they are better positioned to make a difference in the autocratic trajectory. Here is a composite illustration of this vantage point.

The Confidant Who Owes Everything to the Leader

Fresh out of college, David had begun as an intern in his boss's first political campaign. His boss (everyone called

continued

him "the boss") seemed to be "the real deal"—ideological and committed to change.

David brought social media skills to that campaign ahead of his time. He innovated ways of getting out the candidate's message, inspiring young voters to support him, and helping to eke out a narrow victory.

That was six campaigns ago. In the course of those years, David had come on as paid staff in the communications department. Through skill and enthusiasm, he found himself in the inner circle of the boss's first national campaign. While still in his twenties, the influence he was able to exert on the campaign and the candidate surprised even him.

He found that his technical communication skills were well complimented by his sense of reading the electorate's mood, constructing campaign strategies around this, and drafting cross-generational speeches that often rose to the inspirational. The boss turned to him more and more often for his opinion.

Now, in the second full term of his national career, the boss seemed to be changing. He was cracking down on internal dissent with a ferocity that David hadn't seen before. He tried toning down the boss's inflammatory public rhetoric, only to find his drafts heavily edited with red ink.

David grew increasingly uncomfortable with the boss's heavy hand and authoritarian style. But what could he do? The boss had trusted him when no one else had and brought him into the inner circle. He owed him his loyalty. And truthfully, he enjoyed the status he had by being in the inner circle. On a small scale, it mirrored the boss's love of power. He was nobody if the boss threw him out of the circle and word spread that he was no longer in his favor.

David kept up an agreeable face though the discomfort was becoming acute. Was he enabling an increasingly problematic leader? If the boss eventually created his own downfall, what would become of David's reputation for his complicity? How much time was left for him to make his choice?

CONFIDANTS WITH THEIR OWN POWER BASES

The category of inner circle followers with their own power base bears further examination. They have risen to prominence in the world through their own works or, at times, through family relationships. They have power centers independent of the leader's. Regardless of their actual competence, it serves the prototyrant's interests to have them—and their prestige—represented in his administration. Their position may be a product of a negotiation for power sharing or another form of expediency. They rarely enjoy the same trust as those given to others in this circle.

The relationships in this category are highly complex. Because they have a power base, they have more potential to influence the prototyrant, who understands power. If they use that power well, they can interrupt the problematic trajectory of the prototyrant. They would be doing everyone concerned a great service. But why should they do this?

They are often individuals with their own agendas. They

have learned to work behind the scenes to promote their interests without drawing the prototyrant's attention—or so they think. Often, at the earliest opportunity, the prototyrant, who has a paranoid and well-developed sense for anything less than unquestioning loyalty, will remove them when he can do so without paying a significant political price.

Meanwhile, those who have become wary of the prototyrant, and are looking for alternatives, find themselves assessing who might be a better fit with some chance of success. This itself becomes a complex power game, as any of these other players have multiple, competing, and not-always-savory aspects to their political, social, and economic agendas and their personalities. If promoted to ultimate power, any of these problematic dimensions may become more ascendant and wreak equal havoc to those of the displaced prototyrant.

Great caution is needed. Inner circle followers should regard themselves as being in a cage with killer big cats, never losing sight of their whereabouts and machinations. They must maneuver to protect themselves and guard and project their power to keep the cats wary and at bay. This is hardly a formula for highly effective administrations.

Is there one among them with the wile, drive, reputation, and resources to prevail who has an inclination to rule for the greater good? One who will make difficult choices, perhaps harshly, but not with the randomness and utter disregard for all principle, life, and well-being that is at the core of the tyrant?

Make no mistake: If you are privileged to be in the inner

circle, no matter how secure you feel, that security is an illusion. History is replete with examples of a strongman approaching the status of a tyrant, making a fierce example of someone thought to be unassailable. It is often a number two who is garnering popularity that rivals the leader's own or a business mogul whose resources are sufficiently vast to effectively turn on the leader if they choose to do so.

The prototyrant, or the tyrant wanting additional insurance to maintain his status, will deliberately choose the individual of the highest stature to discredit, humiliate, depose, bankrupt, imprison, or eliminate. This sends the unmistakable message that no one is beyond the reach of his displeasure, that the slightest hint of rivalry or lack of acquiescence is sufficient to feel the wrath of the leader. Chairman Mao removed Deng Xiaoping from senior positions below him. When rehabilitated, Deng Xiaoping promoted his protégés Hu Yaobang and Zhao Ziyang to heads of party and government. They, too, were later removed when pushing their agendas.

The Case of Gregor Strasser

I have long been fascinated by the case of Gregor Strasser, an early member of the Nazi Party that eventually elevated Adolph Hitler to chancellor of Germany. Strasser was crucial to Hitler's rise. He was a member of the failed "Beer Hall Putsch," for which he and Hitler and others were tried, convicted, and jailed. When released, Gregor (along with his brother, Otto) used his prodigious organizing skills,

continued

which complemented Hitler's fiery oratorical skills, to transform the Nazi party from its small regional base to a national powerhouse.

Strasser was politically to the left of Hitler, which created a rift and resentment between them. Hitler still needed Strasser to help him gain power, so they were able to reconcile temporarily. When Strasser was offered the position of vice-chancellor of Germany by then Chancellor Franz von Papen, which would have thwarted Hitler's designs on the chancellorship, Hitler reacted furiously. Instead of holding his ground, Strasser chose to retire from politics and return to his former career in pharmacy.

With Hitler's consent, Strasser accepted a director position with a subsidiary of the chemical and pharmaceutical giant IG Farben. He promised to stay out of politics and appeared to have been good to his word. Was this sufficient to protect him from the emerging tyrant?

Soon after Hitler became chancellor, he began ferociously consolidating his power by eliminating all potential rivals. On what became known as the "Night of the Long Knives," hundreds of former but suspect supporters were murdered; the courts fell into line and ignored the extrajudicial killings. Strasser was shot in a main artery and deliberately left to bleed to death in his prison cell. Meanwhile, his brother, Otto, emigrated and wound up living a long life in Nova Scotia before being allowed to repatriate to postwar West Germany.

It cannot be known how history may have been different had the Strasser brothers stood their ground and not folded when facing the emerging tyrant before he consolidated power. But it is a cautionary tale for political elites who find themselves in analogous situations today.

It is only by taking this psychological and historical reality into account that one can make better choices regarding enabling the prototyrant to amass power. It is a fool's belief that once that power is consolidated, the strongman can still be manipulated to serve even a powerful confidant's agenda.

OLD COMRADES

Some confidants were comrades in a progressive or revolutionary movement begun many years prior with noble aspirations to create a "new world." Their leader has now succeeded. Unfortunately, history repeatedly shows that those idealistic leaders with prototyrant characteristics are prone to betray the cause with their abuse of power. If the leader had aspired to the ideals that attracted you to them and failed, they would be remembered as heroes and martyrs. But in success, they too often change. Their sense of themselves, of their superiority, of their infallibility—according to some studies, even their brain functioning—can change.

The British Lord Acton warned that "Power tends to corrupt. Absolute power corrupts absolutely." Note the words *tends to*. This is not inevitable. At the Club of Madrid conference referenced earlier, I met several freedom fighters who became heads of their newly democratic countries and stepped down gracefully when their constitution required doing so. But there are too many cases where this does not occur. Power distorted their perspective, their values, their behaviors. Once they begin to misuse that power, the snowball effect takes hold. As it gains momentum, even those in their most intimate circle, who have struggled or suffered alongside them, find it difficult to slow the snowball's plummeting that is destroying what was worthwhile.

Legions of high-level confidants in history are left betrayed. How did they give their blood, their spirit, their fortune in support of this visionary who became this tyrant? They chose to ignore or minimize the telltale signs of the prototyrant. The lesson: Do not be blind in the early stages of a movement to the flaws and proclivities of the visionary leader. Help them manage those flaws. *Build systems around them to contain those flaws.* And if those flaws show signs of becoming gaping crevasses, find other leaders who serve the movement's values and purpose. Do not walk mindlessly to the point of no return in which those who gave their best are betrayed.

The TICO Times

In a story that is too familiar, Daniel Ortega rose from a revolutionary who overthrew a brutal dictator only to become such a dictator.

Virtually every one of his old comrades who helped free Nicaragua from the reign of Anastasio Somoza is now exiled or imprisoned, if not having already died in jail during Ortega's rule.

"Hugo Torres was a revered Sandinista guerilla [sic] leader that helped overthrow former Nicaraguan dictator Anastasio Somoza and the only revolutionary that participated in the two largest and most successful attacks that overwhelmed Somoza forces and freed many dozens of political prisoners . . .

"Included amongst those prisoners released due to those unprecedented raids was current Nicaraguan dictator Daniel Ortega, the same person that later jailed him until his death. Ortega had been in prison for seven years after robbing a bank.

"After the 1979 revolution, Torres rose to the rank of Chief of National Security and then Army Brigadier General in the new Sandinista government before his retirement in 1998.

"In a video made shortly before his arrest, he stated, 'Forty-six years ago, I risked my life to free Daniel Ortega.' Torres later said those same former comrade revolutionaries have now betrayed the principles they fought for."[1]

FAMILY VALUES

To misquote Tolstoy, all-powerful families are alike, but every family with power conflicts is dysfunctional in its own way.

The leader can hire and fire confidants; they can't fire family. And the family can't fire them. While we like to think of loyalty as an absolute, there are always tensions between competing values. You love your brother, and you love your wife. Your wife and brother don't get along. You're in the middle. How do you maintain your loyalty to both?

The dilemma is only solvable by placing something above loyalty for both of them. Using your very human experience of navigating family dynamics, put yourself in their shoes for a moment. What is that higher loyalty? In the family, it may be a commitment to your children. In the government, it may be a love of country. Whatever you place higher does not make the matter easier, but it gives you other guideposts for making choices.

The leader, who is your brother or father or spouse or daughter or son, is your blood. You are part of the "first family." You revel in the status of your family, having reached the pinnacle of public success. You do not want to lose this exalted place in society or history. The last thing you will do is wash your laundry in full public view. Yet, the laundry is being soiled. The natural higher loyalty for you may be the good name of the family. You are uniquely positioned to protect that.

You know intimately what the family member as leader responds to, what makes them dig in their heels, give or not give an inch. You have access and insight. There is a window in which to use it. When does that window close?

It closes once the leader begins using their power to commit crimes. At that point, their survival depends on those crimes remaining hidden and those aware of the crimes being sidelined and silenced. If you have participated in those crimes, you have become part of the problem. If you have resisted the temptations that were thrown your way, you may still be able to make a difference in the window before abuse of power becomes egregious.

In that window, it is the family member who has the most access and potentially carries the most persuasive weight.

You love that family member too much to see them jeopardize what they have achieved. You care for them and for the family reputation enough to speak what is uncomfortable to say. You love their children and want them always to be proud of their parents. These are higher values than loyalty to the leader, though they propel a deeply loyal act.

You may need to stand in the fire of the leader's anger. The leader may interpret your stance as a massive betrayal. Their fury overwhelms their ability to hear what you are saying. You are family. You cannot be dismissed or fired like every other confidant. If you stand in the fire for as long as needed, retaining your stance, the paroxysm will run its course. You have remained in the window. Now it is time to help the leader—your kin—make the best choice possible, whether it is palatable or difficult to swallow. You have been the final buffer to what would have been a tragic trajectory. You have, in fact, been loyal.

CHAPTER 13

THE CONFIDANT

CIRCLE

Seduced by Power and the Price Paid

.

Being close to power is a form of creating meaning in our lives. It helps us believe we can make a difference. It is enticing to have an opportunity to occupy this privileged position.

We are usually only close enough to one individual who can become *the* leader. Therefore, we are inclined to push that individual to strive for power. We talk to that individual in ways that encourage them and may inflate their sense of inevitability. It is common in Washington, DC, for people close to a senator with national ambition, spoken or not, to start referring to them as "Mr. President." It is a form of flattery but also a speech act that pushes them to think more seriously about entering the race to become the top leader.

This does a disservice to otherwise competent and effective political leaders at their current level. Of course, this doesn't mean we are pushing them to become tyrants! But it is the same dynamic that encourages a would-be tyrant— that stokes their sense of self-importance and inevitability while also feeding the egos of the flatterers.

The Indian scholar B.R. Ambedkar, who oversaw the drafting of the Indian constitution, observed that "in politics . . . hero worship is a sure road to degradation and to eventual dictatorship."

Invoking John Stuart Mills, he warned his countrymen not to "lay their liberties at the feet of even a great man, or to trust him with powers which enable him to subvert their institutions."

Followers must be cautious and prudent about the leader they are creating, for indeed, it is they who are creating the leader. Intimate followers even more so. Creating a leader who leads to serve can bring meaning to all of their lives. Creating a leader who is fulfilling a fantasy of invincibility and dominance is a recipe for spawning tyrants.

VULNERABILITY—ELITE FOLLOWERS AND THE ILLUSION OF SAFETY

Russian and Chinese history for the last hundred years shows that the dominant figure of any time frequently targeted and undermined their close allies. Being in the inner circle does not confer safety for a number of reasons:

The tyrannical leader is always wary of those who gain too much visibility. They are potential rivals. As often as not, ways will be found to deflate or eliminate them as a perceived threat.

When things go wrong, the leader must shift blame to someone else of stature—often someone in the inner circle. These privileged followers "die on their sword" for the leader.

Those in the inner circle often share their leaders' lust for power and fear of being displaced. The infighting, backstabbing, and undermining of each other is endemic in all but the rarest of these circles.

Being so close to the authoritarian ruler, they, more than others, see their leader's feet of clay, yet somehow, must disguise this perception from the leader. Doing so is a nearly impossible feat that generates "tells," which the leader detects and eventually acts on.

Most tyrannical leaders, despite years of being in power, eventually are deposed if they don't die first. Those who served them most closely are highly suspect and often receive the wrath of the people, the new leaders, or the courts once the prototyrant no longer needs to be feared. Confidants do well to weigh this range of risks when choosing to stand up to the prototyrant or to harness themselves to his fate.

The story of Seneca the Younger (Roman philosopher and statesman, 4BC–AD65) and Nero (the fifth Roman emperor,

continued

AD37–AD68) illustrates the grave danger of working close to the tyrant despite being a favorite.

Seneca was the son of a wealthy Roman family. His life intersected with Rome's famous and infamous emperors—Caligula, Claudius, and Nero. Claudius banished Seneca from Rome on charges of impropriety, during which time he established himself as a moral philosopher of some stature. When he returned to Rome, he married a wealthy woman and built a powerful circle of friends, including Burrus, a prominent official of the Roman guard. One of his pupils was the future emperor Nero. Clearly, Seneca was a power in his own right.

When Nero became emperor, Seneca and Burrus were elevated to his inner circle and became among his favorites. They are credited with influencing positive government reforms, but their position placed them at odds with Nero's domineering mother, who increasingly provoked his ire.[1]

While historical accounts vary, it is generally thought that Seneca and Burrus had to, at least, condone her murder, if not themselves implement Nero's orders to eliminate her. Nero's subsequent guilt is said to have weighed on him and distorted his relations with Burrus and Seneca. When Burrus died, Seneca, feeling the isolation of his position, retired. This did not sufficiently satisfy Nero's paranoia of opposition. He ordered Seneca to end his own life by taking poison, which he did. We may wonder, what were his final thoughts?

POWER AND CRIMES

If the leader commits crimes while accruing or exercising power, it vastly compounds the problem of letting go of power. Fear of retribution and being held accountable makes holding onto power paramount.

They say that misery loves company. They might also say that criminals love criminals. Not only is committing crimes for or with the leader a rite of passage for the confidants of the prototyrant, but also a strategy to bind the confidants closer. Just as the criminal leader is no longer safe letting go of political power, neither are his criminal cronies. Soldiers with their backs to a raging river fight harder. Political criminals with their backs to a war tribunal, charges of crimes against humanity, a lifetime of incarceration, or a hangman's noose will fight to the death to escape those fates. The prototyrant ensures it is not just him who faces this fate if they allow him to lose.

What would you do if you were among the inner circle and pressured to engage in what are clearly crimes?

If the leader persuades you to commit a crime, or you commit a crime on the leader's behalf to serve what you believe is in your and their interest, you are compromised. This will make it almost impossible to leave the leader's orbit or to withstand the pressure to commit further criminal acts for the leader. They can use your transgression against you, if convenient, and their enemies certainly will use it against you, targeting you before they can get to him. You become bound to the leader even as the ship goes down or deserves to be sunk.

To retain your freedom of choice, you must evade the pressure to commit an actionable crime—not the fourth or fifth time, but *the first time*. This is the critical juncture. Once you cross the line, it perversely is in your apparent interest to continue crossing lines. If you resist and the leader already has "the goods on you," you are in the grips of blackmail. The first time is when the roads diverge, and taking the wrong one doesn't end well.

It is here that whatever favor you enjoy with the leader must be played upon. Reframe the instruction for the leader as leaving them more vulnerable. What is it the leader is trying to achieve (besides implicating you)? What other ways can you help them achieve that? The leader may also be at a junction. The more they use criminal activity, the more ammunition their enemies have. The more confidants they ensnare in criminal activity, the more lackeys there are who can eventually turn on the leader with incriminating evidence.

This stance is, of course, not without risk. If the prototyrant is a sociopath, they will view your resistance as disloyalty, and you will begin to experience the lashes they can dole out. This is a risk that must be taken, as it is the only stance that may interrupt the trajectory of the prototyrant while saving yourself. If taking the risk produces harsh penalties, it is proof that somehow you must extricate yourself from the reach of the leader, or you must begin identifying allies who will assist in constraining or derailing the leader.

The perks of being close to power have been great. The risks are greater.

Watergate Defendants

All Americans of a certain age can tell you about Watergate—the illegal break-in at the Democratic campaign office and its cover-up, resulting in the unprecedented resignation of a US president, Richard M. Nixon.

How many know that sixty-nine government officials were charged and forty-eight were found guilty in courts of law? Nixon himself was granted a controversial pardon by President Gerald Ford, who succeeded him. However, five of Nixon's closest aides, including the attorney general of the United States, served prison time, including his chief of staff, who is typically one of a political leader's closest confidants.[2]

In this case, the rule of law worked. A descent down the slippery slope from legitimate leader to rule by autocracy was interrupted, though with significant cost to the nation while the investigations and trials proceeded. These confidants might have saved their leader's presidency and themselves prison time if they had prevented the criminal act or used their access to counsel against the disastrous cover-up. A cautionary tale for all those close to power, which we will examine further in the next chapter.

AN APPROACH TO THE PROBLEM OF POWER AND MONEY

It is highly likely that an authoritarian leader and those closest to that leader will use their power for personal enrichment. There are exceptions, but this is so common in human affairs that it may be necessary to work within this culture, even if not personally engaging in or condoning it.

There are ways these actors can increase their well-being without flagrantly crossing lines of propriety. For example, if they want a road built to their summer dacha, make sure the road also serves surrounding communities who need to transport their goods to market. They can invest in businesses that may have an unfair advantage but do not violate criminal statutes. If their project of remaining in power is not successful—which it often is not, they have a way out that leaves them financially secure and able to protect themselves without being subject to national and international prosecution.

Not only is this good for the circle of confidants, but it is also good for the prototyrant whom they serve. Why bet all their money on staying in power when history demonstrates that only a minority of dictators or tyrants achieve this for their natural lifetime? More often, they are overthrown by a popular uprising or military coup or defeated by other nations when they overplay their hand. Confidants serve both the leader and themselves well by creating the potential for a strategic and comfortable exit. Though not necessarily part of their motivation, they potentially also serve the nation by having created an acceptable "off-ramp" that avoids the paroxysms of displacing entrenched tyrannical power.

TEMPERANCE

By reason of proximity and potential for influence, confidants have an elevated moral responsibility to check the progression of tyrannical power. The prototyrannical leader expects total support for their agenda and complete loyalty to their person. Yet this is not what they or the polity needs.

Exceptional followership in Circles 1 and 2 requires less-than-lockstep thinking with the prototyrant's impulses, and the skills to extract concessions from the power-drenched leader. They need to inject temperance into the autocrat's style and playbook.

There is a great art to this, as no leader, and especially no autocratic leader, will long tolerate continual advice to tone down, proceed slowly, or ease up. They have built their success on action, risk-taking, and daring to go beyond the boundaries that constrain others.

The art involves effectiveness in executing most of the leader's demands while reserving their cautions for the more outrageous ones. Assuming you still feel this leader can serve some greater, prosocial purpose (despite their egregious flaws), save the brakes for the battles that must be fought and won. If, despite judicious use, you have burned out the brakes, it may be time to cease following and find a way to extricate yourself from the runaway train safely.

An Autocrat Whisperer

A former colleague and friend of mine had been quite close to a larger-than-life leader who had a vision for transforming

continued

the world. This leader had created a global network of organizations that were executing his vision. His methods were nonviolent but increasingly authoritarian, doctrinaire, and punitive—a nongovernmental prototyrant.

This colleague was one of his senior aides, who was responsible for public relations. I asked her how she would tame his worst impulses. She told me that, at some point in the conversation, when he was holding forth on what he wanted done, she would introduce a better idea, telling him that was "what she gathered he meant." In other words, she always kept it *his* idea, which his inflated egoism required. Sometimes, this worked. When she ceased being sufficiently influential and was no longer willing to follow, she managed to extricate herself—not always a choice available to a confidant of a political prototyrant.

MODERATING THE EFFECT OF PROTOTYRANNICAL CONFIDANTS

There is a unique challenge for those followers in the first circle who want to modulate a leader's prototyrannical behavior.

There will be one or more other followers in that inner circle who are as prone to tyrannical behavior as the prime leader. As a result, they will earn the trust of the leader, who sees them as an extension of himself. If another follower attempts to bring the prototyrant to a more reasonable course of action, the prototyrannical *follower* will undermine them.

Therefore, the first strategic action of the confidant attempting to modulate the leader's behavior is neutralizing the influence of the prototyrannical *follower*. This entails its risks. One can try engaging the dangerous follower in their transformation, but the rewards for their behavior make this extremely difficult to do.

The most likely method of success in diminishing their influence on the leader is to identify a flagrant flaw that discredits them to the leader or clear proof of their self-aggrandizing motives. Bringing this, directly or indirectly, to the attention of the leader sows distrust in their original assessment of the destructive confidant.

Yes, this is a distasteful game of inner circle politics, but that is exactly the game being played against oneself by the prototyrannical follower. The game must be engaged if you are to be effective. It is not a matter of the ends justifying the means, as the means, in this case, are not harmful.

Protective Factors

"You can't build all of these leadership values, knowledge, and skills without also building the protective factors so that when someone gets in the arena, they know when to step out, they know when to step forth, they know when to fight, they know when to play."
—JOHN DUGAN, PhD[3]

At times, this prototyrannical follower is even more dangerous than the leader. Just as followers create leaders, they may be creating the prototyrant in their own image and to serve their purpose. They may have an outsized effect that defies rationality. The classic historical example is the monk

Rasputin's role in the downfall of the ill-served Romanov tsars in early twentieth-century Russia, destroying the potential for reform that other confidants in the court were urging.

Colin Powell

A more contemporary example that not everyone will agree with is the coterie of followers around then-US President George W. Bush. Post 9/11, several influential confidants, arguably led by then-vice president Dick Cheney, were pushing the president to invade Iraq. The pretext was that the tyrannical Iraqi president, Saddam Hussein, was secretly hoarding weapons of mass destruction. The underlying agenda was greater security and control of the oil-rich region and their gravely mistaken vision that the Iraqi people would welcome the invaders. This would create the conditions for transforming the Middle East into thriving democracies and counter the graver threat posed by neighboring theocratic Iran, which was fiercely anti-American.

Then-Secretary of State General Colin Powell, who under President George H. W. Bush oversaw the earlier successful armed intervention against Iraq's invasion of the oil-rich country of Kuwait, was not convinced. He persuaded the president, sometimes referred to as Bush II, to seek the support of the UN General Assembly before initiating military action. When Bush did so, and the Cheney wing of confidants kept pushing for invasion, Powell was outmaneuvered and sidelined. He did not serve as Bush's secretary of state in his second administration. Twenty years later, the region is still in turmoil.

THE PROBLEM OF
INSTITUTIONALIZED CORRUPTION

Institutionalized corruption is the seemingly unsolvable dilemma of political followership at the highest levels. The truly tyrannical leader knows that the bond of fear is only half the cement to keep followers in line. The other half is the reward of sanctioned corruption.

This makes the risk-reward ratio of supporting or opposing the leader the proverbial no-brainer from the self-interest perspective. Oppose the leader and risk ruin, support the leader, and be rewarded handsomely with privilege. The incentives are so totally aligned for supporting the leader that only a fool or a hero would oppose them. Is there any solution?

Possibly, there are two. The first is that a member of the inner circle (or someone near it) has equally powerful ambition as the rapidly rising prototyrant. They may take a gambit of using charges of corruption as the vehicle to depose the prototyrant, just as he uses charges of corruption to keep political rivals off the ballot in performative democracies. This is not, of course, without its risks. Other confidants who benefit from the corruption are likely to rally around the leader and isolate the reformer unless the leader is so mercurial and vicious that other confidants' self-preservation instincts support the prototyrant's removal. Even if the gambit is successful, power will work its corruptive nature on the replacement unless institutional safeguards to mitigate corruption are created in this window of opportunity.

The second is that a rare reformer arises who is following

a different siren call. For reasons that go to the inscrutable heart of occasional human goodness found at the governance level, they hold equal or greater power to the source of corruption and terror. The risks are so great that one cannot look to the calculus of self-interest to explain their motivation, except perhaps to the motivation of their legacy. While this book was being edited, we witnessed a contemporary example in Alexei Navalny, the courageous Russian dissident who had been attempting for years to expose the corruption of Russian President Vladimir Putin. Navalny was found dead at the age of forty-six in the prison camp in which he was detained.[4]

There is no point in my giving counsel to this rare reformer; their guidance comes from a deeper internal connection to this intangible counterweight to evil. However, counsel can be given to other followers in Circles 1 or 2 who witness the emergence of an individual manifesting this ethical presence. Recognize that the calculus of self-interest may put one's life at a crossroads—inextricable entanglement with a corrupt regime or a chance to free oneself from its grip. Supporting the courageous confidant and the institutional reforms they champion may allow him to succeed and give all circles of followers a chance to reclaim the healthy trajectory of their lives and their public service.

DILEMMAS FACED BY THE CLOSEST ADVISOR

In democracies, the role of advisor to the president or prime minister or other elected official is to support them; they are the elected voice of the people or their party. Specifically, it is to support them in implementing the policy platform on which they were elected and to help them retain office long enough to do so successfully. These two mandates, at times, conflict with each other, and the counselor helps the leader navigate these conflicts.

Advisors know they have a responsibility to give the leader their best counsel, even their divergent views. However, almost all are continuously reading the leader's physical and verbal cues of openness or disapproval in response to their input. In response to this, their counsel often gets softened or silenced—not by the leader directly, but by their own internal need to stay in the leader's favor.

I recall hearing about aides meeting with then-president George H. W. Bush—certainly not a political leader with tyrannical tendencies. Nevertheless, aides would watch his jawline. When it began to clench, they knew his patience was wearing thin toward an argument they were making in favor of a course of action. It was a signal to wrap it up and get off that line of argument rather than wait to be verbally shut down.

Advisors do not want to lose personal influence with the leader and fear they may do so if they persist in an unwelcome vein of questioning or counsel. They may self-censor or state unpopular views that they believe are critical to the common good in subdued tones so they are not ousted from the circle. Getting oneself disinvited would leave a vacuum to be filled by those whose views are closer to the misinformed or fallacious ones of the leader. The skillful confidant is, in part, making a self-interested calculation and, in part, a political calculation.

Moral guideposts can help confidants in these precarious situations. Guideposts, or principles, can inform when to push and when to withdraw in service of influencing policy. If these confidants confuse their ego and agenda with their objective counsel to the leader, they do him and the electorate a disservice. Advisors need to differentiate between their impulse to be in control when this is not their duty (as they are not the ones elected) and their responsibility to give forthright counsel while appropriately subordinating their preferences to the leader's preference. It can be difficult to discern the difference between these postures and how to navigate them with self-awareness and accountability.

To some degree, this becomes a team endeavor. Each confidant can help the other examine where the appropriate line is. Ultimately, the counselor may need to withdraw to a place of reflection about what seems the most appropriate way to serve. These delicate dynamics are not easily subject to simplified rules when highly contingent judgment is required in each circumstance.

COMPLEXITY OF MOTIVATION

Because of the complex motivations in the first circle of followers, those in the second circle or even the third circle need to be particularly strategic in what information they feed to these agenda-driven followers with extraordinary access to the ultimate decision-maker.

They must not withhold information that would be of

value to this first circle of followers, for doing that would soon cost them their position when detected. However, they must be thoughtful about how they frame the information they are providing.

When possible, they should present the information in ways that support its use in promoting positive values. They should avoid the temptation of framing the information in ways they believe ingratiate them to the first circle by inflaming its negative aspects.

The very senior confidants to whom they send that information rarely have time to examine and vet what they are given closely. Therefore, they may use it in ways that worsen existing and future conditions, aggravating the harm to others.

It must be made clear up front why the information is important to the leader and to their close confidant. It is usually expected that the information will be accompanied by several options for response to the situation. Without overselling your preference, highlight the ways in which that option serves both policy and political interests, which the confidant can use to persuade the leader to make choices that are more beneficial than harmful.

THE GREATEST DANGERS

There are two windows of great danger to which the inner circle must stay alert.

The first window is that of success. As the political leader with prototyrannical proclivity achieves success, their confidence increases, as happens for all of us. But theirs enters the territory of hubris.

Because a prototyrant erodes the capabilities of rival power centers, he begins to rely increasingly on his instincts and advice. When these are successful, they become a reinforcing loop. Initially, close confidants are elated: Their man is proving to be the success they believed in and are working for. His fortunes are rising, and so are theirs.

What the confidants may not see is that, as this occurs, the prototyrant also begins to rely less on them. They notice their advice is no longer being sought or received when given. It is not that their advice is necessarily good or bad; rather, it is a form of diffusion of perspective that will tend to consider more factors than the leader relying on their own limited perspective.

This is a difficult time for the confidant to call into question a leader's choices. He is successful! There is greater reluctance to question him and greater resistance on his part to being questioned. This is so central to the descent into tyrannical rule that every circle of confidants would be well advised to discuss this dynamic *before* successes begin mounting. How will they, the inner circle (including the leader), guard against this narrowing of perspective in decision-making on the most consequential issues? It is not that the leader is obligated to follow their counsel but to recognize the tendency to discount it—and to misattribute success to their own supposed infallibility.

The counselor who cautions this can find themselves isolated and unsupported by their peers and erstwhile rivals if they wait until the success train gains a head of steam. The time to name this and establish norms is at, or before, the first hint of the danger of success.

Putin

Russian President Vladimir Putin's success with invading Georgia and Crimea earlier in the new century made him wildly overconfident about invading the heart of Ukraine in 2022, resulting in a series of embarrassing early defeats and the strengthening of the NATO alliance he had sought to undermine. Whether or not Russia recovers from these early setbacks, Putin tarnished his own "invincible" image and came close to a showdown with one of his mercenary leaders who took the brazen act of marching toward the capitol in protest of the army's lackluster performance.

Putin would have done well to study how Adolph Hitler's overreliance on earlier successes in Western Europe led him to break his nonaggression treaty and invade the Soviet Union in WWII, the catalyst for his ultimate downfall.

The second great danger is the prospect of impending defeat. The threat is directly proportional to the paranoid state of mind of the leader and the degree of crimes they have committed in securing and retaining power. The stakes of losing power are too high. This danger is perceived by the leader as being so great that they become willing to risk any gamble—regardless of the costs to others—to maintain their hold on power. If the inner circle has participated in those crimes, they will reinforce the desperate stand and actions of the leader.

The first antidote to this is, of course, not colluding with the leader in crimes. But some things cannot be changed retroactively. What is the role of the closest confidants in this situation? It is to recognize when a prospective defeat is approaching and to begin identifying the off-ramps for the leader and themselves. We have again entered the window of possibility for interrupting the trajectory to tyrannical rule and ultimate disaster.

Saddam Hussein

Acting *before* the prototyrant has consolidated power is crucial. When the United States and its allies were preparing to invade Iraq based on the false information of its stockpiling weapons of mass destruction, one of Premier Saddam Hussein's cabinet suggested that perhaps it would be best for him to take an administrative leave for a few weeks to mollify the US. The window had long ago closed. The following day, the minister's dismembered body was delivered to his family. Absolute power had fully worked its corrupting influence. A different strategy would have been needed in order to succeed or even to survive.[5]

Intimate counselors, including family, can quietly begin envisioning exit ramps from the misuse of power, or even from political power itself, while minimizing the consequences to the leader or themselves. This will require deep knowledge of the other confidants in regards to who will share their concerns and maintain their confidences as they generate ideas for a "soft landing" for the regime. At some point, this will require the further risk of bringing in key players from the elite circle to support that plan. For this to be a success, it will require courage, savvy, a good faith intent to reduce broad harm, and pragmatic self-interest to mitigate adverse consequences. This is the correct role for the inner circle to play, but it may need to play it along with other circles, as we will see in the chapter on coalitions of followers.

PRESIDENT FOR LIFE

In the progression from democracy to dictatorship, the political sine qua non is the elected leader altering or abrogating the constitution to enable them to serve as president for life. It is hard to claim this is still a representative democracy, regardless of the performative trappings the regime may keep in place.

Alexander Lukashenko

The country of Belarus achieved independence from the former Soviet Union in 1991. In 1994, Alexander Lukashenko was elected president and has served ever since as its one-man center of power.

The 1994 election was generally considered free and fair, the first and last such election in independent Belarus. Shortly afterward, Lukashenko started to consolidate power and dismantle institutions.[6]

As of this book's writing, Chinese President Xi Jinping had broken with tradition and forced the Chinese governing apparatus and its rubber-stamp parliament to enable him to serve a third consecutive five-year term, opening the way for him to rule as paramount leader for life. He received a unanimous 2,952 votes in Parliament, followed by a standing ovation. (Talk about no one sitting on their hands or folding their arms across their chest!)

While the role of the president (or state chair) in China is ceremonial, Xi Jinping simultaneously occupies both of the real power positions in the Chinese politburo, the head of the party and the army. These were also conferred on him for a third term. Apparently, the window for interrupting this dictatorial ascent has firmly closed. However, Xi Jinping is certainly not the only head of state and government to have broken existing norms and potentially cast themselves in their role for life.

A well-known example occurred in one of the world's oldest democracies—the United States of America. The drafters of the United States Constitution debated on whether to place a term limit on the office of the president and chose not to do so. The first president, George Washington, after serving two terms, voluntarily refrained from running for a third term. While he was tired of long years of public service and wanted to return to his comfortable plantation—well served by over three hundred enslaved men and women—he is also credited with not wanting to implicitly recreate the position of king, which the newly founded nation had fought to free itself from.

Whatever Washington's primary reasons, his example became the norm, reinforced when the nation's second president, Thomas Jefferson, also declined to run for a third term. This norm served the nation well from when Washington left office in 1797 until the election of Franklin Delano Roosevelt to a third term in office, which began in 1941. That is a norm that lasted just shy of 150 years. Why was it flaunted by Roosevelt?

We have seen the relationship between leading, following, and context. The context at the time was fertile for someone perceived to be a strong leader. The nation had come through a foundation-shaking decade of economic depression that was just beginning to end as it built its war production capacity to supply the English in their mortal battle with Nazi Germany. The threat of totalitarian regimes in Europe hung over the collective psyche. A strong case could be made for reelecting the president who presided over the conomic recovery and the resistance to totalitarianism. But the debate was fierce over whether even this was enough to flout what had become a deep democratic tradition. What role did his confidants play?

Harold Ickes came to the inner circle of the democrat Franklin Delano Roosevelt when Roosevelt sought a progressive Republican cabinet member after his first election. Ickes proceeded to serve in Roosevelt's cabinet longer than any other secretary, eventually holding the second-longest record in US history. He was canny and politically effective.

Ickes's background included a history of championing social reform. This did not suggest that he favored tyrannical rule. But he adopted a combative stance against presidential term limits. When the question of running for a third term arose, Roosevelt somewhat coyly announced that he would only do so if his political party drafted him as the nominee. With war in Europe looming, using this as its rationale, the party nominated him on the first ballot.[7]

While I am not implying that Roosevelt was pursuing a consolidation of power similar to the one Xi Jinping pursued, we can see their actions exist along a certain continuum. After serving the third term in 1944, with World War II still raging and US and allied forces driving back the Germans, Roosevelt was nominated for a fourth term. Ickes and other confidants masked his failing health from the public. Roosevelt died in office eighty-two days after his fourth inauguration. Unintentionally, he had served as president for life.

When the 22nd amendment, imposing term limits on the US presidency, was proposed, Ickes characterized it as a "sinister plot on the part of anti-social agencies to frighten them (the people) into mutilating their own precious democracy to the advantage of those who have exploited the people and always will."[8] Using this incendiary language, he was making a classic argument: democracy requires that the people decide, without limits, whom they want for president. However, the Constitution already imposed limits on age and birthplace, and it was amended after the US Civil War to exclude insurrectionists.

This fiercely loyal confidant failed to see what many others saw as a dangerous constitutional path to potential dictatorship. Despite objections, what had been a norm became embedded in the constitution, receiving significant bipartisan support in Congress and ratification by forty-one states, easily clearing the required threshold. The 22nd amendment became law on Feb 27, 1951, and three-quarters of a century later, it remains a guardrail against the usurpation of power by a prototyrant and his circle of confidants.

CONFIDANTS	SUMMARY
Available Information	Autocrat's musings, rantings, strategies, and instructions
Incentives to Follow	Loyalty, perks, and rewards of power, consequences of loss of power
Vulnerability	Loyalty to the person, not the office
Risks	Complicity in illegal acts, becoming a scapegoat or a danger to the autocrat
Communication Channels	Private conversations, personal contact info, inner circle briefings, and eyes-only communications
Courage Needed	Working with others to curtail tyrannical inclinations
Power to Influence	Last person in the room, final touches on communications and policies

CHAPTER 14

COALITIONS OF

FOLLOWERS

How They Stop a Tyrant

.

> "Coercive power is the curse of the universe,
> coactive power, the enrichment and
> advancement of every human soul."
> —MARY PARKER FOLLETT, Leadership Theorist

THE INTERDEPENDENCE OF THE CIRCLES OF FOLLOWERS

For the purpose of better understanding the nature and role of followers at different levels of proximity to the political leader, I have treated each with a significant amount of distinctiveness.

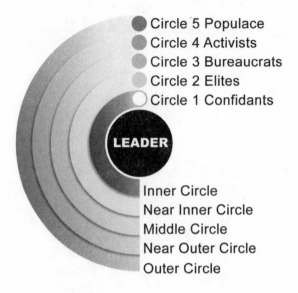

Circle 5 Populace
Circle 4 Activists
Circle 3 Bureaucrats
Circle 2 Elites
Circle 1 Confidants

LEADER

Inner Circle
Near Inner Circle
Middle Circle
Near Outer Circle
Outer Circle

They all generally have motives for following or opposing the leader, incentives and disincentives for doing one or
the other, different access to information and communication channels, and different types of power to bring to the
leader-follower dynamic. Yet, in the world of political activity, they rarely work fully independent of each other.

By the very nature of politics, a field exists or is created of
overlapping interests and energies and of resonant or discor-
dant information. At any given point, different participants
within this field will experience alignment with the political
dynamic or discomfort and resistance to it. Where that discomfort and resistance begins and with what intensity will
vary by the situation.

When that misaligned energy fails to be reconciled to
the political leadership, it sends out ripples that interact
with the incipient discontent in other parts of a circle and
between circles of political followers. A harmonic dissonance

occurs that requires a response by the leadership or, in the case of an intransigent prototyrant, elicits forceful suppression, crossing the threshold to a full-blown tyrant.

The buildup of this energy contains the potential for reform of the political leadership or its removal and replacement. The ideal in most cases is reform, if possible. Replacement offers no guarantee of betterment. If a political vacuum is created, it may be filled by an even stronger prototyrant. Vladimir Lenin was ruthless in forging the former Soviet Union; after his incapacitation and death, his successor, Josef Stalin, and his policies resulted in millions more deaths. Reform is preferred, but only so long as there is a credible movement toward it; left too long, consolidation of repressive power closes the window for meaningful improvement.

No master strategy is needed, either for reform or replacement. The energy for either will emerge from the realities and perceptions of the political field itself. However, those in each circle do well to pay attention to the signs and directions of the emerging energy and rise to contribute to the correction or replacement of the prototyrannical forces at work.

Reform Is the Preferred Goal

Let me be emphatic and state again that the first line of approach is to assume it may be possible to interrupt the political leader's prototyrannical tendencies.

We all have these tendencies within us, as do all political leaders. In our personal growth, our task is to be self-aware and manage these impulses while fostering the prosocial aspects of our character. In societal dynamics, it is the task of the followers around the emerging prototyrant to be aware of the danger, and require the leader to manage those aspects of their character better.

The earlier we do this, the better chance of success. It's the "child and the hot stove" loop: Touch the stove, get burned; don't do that again. For the leader: exert belligerent autocratic pressure, meet unremitting disapproval; don't do that again. Find better ways to make things happen.

I worked with a congressional office in which the congresswoman was a rising star with an eye toward future party leadership. She was ambitious, dynamic, and fiercely outspoken. Her legislative director had been with her from the beginning and was her most trusted aide. One day, she flew off the handle, berating him loudly for not having understood what she was trying to do. He quietly said to her, "You know that I admire you and believe in your agenda. I will do anything to help you succeed. But if you ever talk to me that way again, you will have my resignation on your desk." She never spoke to him that way again.

Setting these boundaries is foremost the responsibility of the confidant circle. But it is available to every circle in its own form. In the face of a policy shift that weakens democratic norms, activists and the populace may flood into the streets, requiring a policy rollback. Bureaucrats can fire off rock-solid analyses of the consequences of the shift. Elites may get on talk programs, exposing or even cleverly ridiculing the new policy, further raising resistance to it among the populace. Political campaign contributions can plummet, creating their own "hot stove" experience for the leader.

In New York City, where the subways are electrified, this is spoken of as "the third rail" effect. The politician learns that touching a particular issue—that "rail"—will create a painful electrical shock that may well be fatal. If the third rail effect is targeted to actions that weaken democratic norms, reform is possible.

Early Resistance Is the Key

It can't be emphasized enough that early resistance is required to emerging tyrannical behavior—*not just when the leader reaches the apex of the political pyramid, but at every stage of their ascendance.* If a leader is allowed to run roughshod over others when they are a precinct head, party leader, cabinet minister, or a chief of staff, God help the State when they are supreme leader.

There is nothing like success to cement beliefs and behavior patterns. "If I were ruthless and successful as mayor, I will be more ruthless as governor. This is what got me where I am." It is the wrong lesson. A combination of skills, circumstances, and follower support got them where they are. But, if they believe it was their ruthlessness, then they will exert more of that on each new rung of the ladder.

This resistance requires the courage of the individual. But if the individual is left on their own to speak truth to power, they will be cut down to size by the prototyrant. Early resistance includes early support for the one who is speaking what others are feeling. Yes, there are risks to this. But these are the principles:

- The closer you get to the power center, the more you are called to find the courage that spoken resistance requires.

- Letting tyrannical behavior go unchecked strengthens the prototyrant's belief in the effectiveness of their way of dominating situations.

- Unchecked, this behavior ends in the carnage that tyrants create with the power of the state at their disposal.

The Case History Problem

There is a problem of analyzing examples of interrupting the progression of an autocrat to a political tyrant. If we are successful in interrupting this progression, the autocrat never becomes a tyrant, so we don't know if the case we are studying is a true example. Maybe the autocrat would not have become a tyrant anyway. If Hitler had been stopped when he broke the existing treaty and sent a military force into the Rhineland, he might never have become the tyrant responsible for some sixty million deaths during World War II. We could not use that as a case example of how much destruction was averted, as that destruction would not have occurred.

Yet examining a case is instructive. So, we do the next best thing: We take an example of a political leader who began misusing power and was caught before they could morph into a tyrant. We assume, if given the chance, they might have become a tyrant and see what we can learn from them. That is what we will do in this chapter, which integrates the actions of the circles of followers.

Conformists, Colluders, and Courageous Followers

For the purposes of this summary, I am drawing on the work of my colleague Alain de Sales, whose doctoral thesis takes a comprehensive dive into how to stop a destructive leader, whether in government, industry, or any other sphere of organized human activity.[1] Like this book, he focuses on the role of followers. I introduced his three types of follower behavior earlier in the book and will summarize them again here:

- *Conformist followers* go about their business, falling in line with whatever dictates emanate from the toxic leader.

- *Colluder followers* actively enable the toxic leader, even amplifying their toxicity.

- *Courageous followers* seek ways to counteract the toxicity, including removing the destructive leader if necessary.

De Sales cites the work of Anthony Padilla regarding the "toxic triangle," which consists of the destructive leader, the enabling followers, and the opportunity that exists in the current environment for a destructive leader to emerge. This, again, echoes the elements of Barbara Kellerman's leadership system: leader, followers, context.

Note that in my use of the term *prototyrant*, I am suspending judgment as to whether the leader is explicitly toxic. Instead, I am focusing on the window in which destructive tendencies emerge and can potentially be interrupted or transformed. De Sales's perspectives are germane to doing this. Rather than introducing the reader to all of his observations and somewhat unique terminology, I focus on those aspects that help us understand how the different circles of followers can work synergistically to thwart the trajectory of the potential tyrant. De Sales' claim is that individual followers cannot themselves interrupt that trajectory; organic or intentional coalitions of followers must use specific strategies that leverage their combined power.

De Sales uses three case histories to make these points. One comes from the political world, which is the domain of this book. I will use that to summarize his salient points and tie together the roles of the different circles of followers in interrupting a tyrannical progression. His case examines the US role in the Vietnam War under the presidencies of Lyndon Johnson and Richard Nixon. I particularly like this because it is clearly nonpartisan. We cannot allow partisanship to close our eyes to potential tyrannical behavior from any political quarter.

De Sales cites the academic literature that bases a definition of destructive leadership on its outcomes, not intent. In this book, we are more interested in intent that can be detected and interrupted *before* producing destructive outcomes.

Lyndon Johnson—Destructive Leader?

De Sales classifies former US President Lyndon Johnson (November 22, 1963, upon the assassination of President John F. Kennedy, until January 20, 1969) as a destructive leader. I characterize him as a flawed leader, with important positive domestic policy accomplishments and an unsavory foreign policy with deeply traumatic results. This is an important distinction, as it represents the challenges of too hastily labeling a leader as a destructive figure. For our purposes, we are focusing not on acts with destructive consequences (as terrible as these may be) but on the signs the leader is moving from isolated destructive acts to entrenched tyrannical rule.

While Johnson is well known for his personal bullying behavior, he ultimately was temperamentally a creature of the US Senate where he served for many years and learned the necessity of bringing others along if anything is to be accomplished in a representative system of governance. Listening to many of the eight hundred hours of tapes of his meetings and phone conversations from the White House, made with recording devices he installed in the Oval Office, illustrates this. We are struck by how continuously he reaches out to former Senate colleagues and to members of his cabinet, as well as his inner circle of advisors, and to media and other elites. Flattering, querying, commiserating, cajoling—not the behavior of the prototyrant but of a skilled politician.

Despite this, whether because of the status of his office, the magnitude of his presence, or both, he did not create a culture of easily questioning or contradicting him. This resulted in followers in the bureaucratic, elite, and confidant circles inflating and misrepresenting to him the progress the US was making in the Vietnam War that he inherited from his predecessor and significantly escalated. He, in turn, made terrible choices regarding the prosecution of the war and its representation to the American public. Meanwhile, the populace circle and the activist circle, relying on other means of information and channels of communication, were increasingly ramping up resistance to the war and his policies.

If Johnson did have prototyrannical tendencies, they were not ascendant. Prototyrants cling to power, regardless of the cost to themselves or others. Johnson was worn down and personally defeated by the stresses of national discord and the war itself and chose not to run for a second full term as president. The withdrawal of support and drumbeat of opposition from the outer circles interrupted whatever autocratic impulse he may have harbored. As they should.

Courage in the Circles of Followers

Before examining the toxic characteristics of the subsequent US president, Richard Nixon (January 1969 to August 9, 1974, when he resigned), de Sales introduces a cast of players he considers to have been courageous followers who took action to interrupt further abuses of power by both Johnson and Nixon.

The first of these is, on the face of it, a surprising choice— Defense Secretary Robert McNamara. Many in his day, including me, viewed him as one of the architects of the escalation of the Vietnam War, beginning in the Kennedy era and accelerating under President Johnson. While this appears initially to be true, de Sales documents a change of perspective on McNamara's part and ineffective private attempts to persuade Johnson to reverse course.

Ultimately, McNamara was faced with the dilemma that while in the president's cabinet (Circle 2 elites, and arguably Circle 1 confidantes, since he worked closely with Johnson), he could not publicly announce his change of perspective. Instead, he became the face of the war. He had the option and chose not to use it, of resigning and speaking candidly about his new assessment, which would have been the most courageous choice.

Nevertheless, intentionally or not, McNamara made a large (if not explicitly intended) contribution to turning public opinion (populace, Circle 5) against the war. De Sales documents that McNamara commissioned the Vietnam Study Task Force, the creators of what became known as the Pentagon Papers, which exposed the reality of the futility of the war. The task force was comprised of thirty-six researchers hired from a wide range of bureaucratic circles, as well as professional scholars and staff from a nonprofit research institution (the RAND Corporation). The latter included military strategist Daniel Ellsberg.

Ellsberg, acting within the bureaucratic structure (Circle 3 followers), saw the falsehoods the Johnson administration was feeding to the US Congress and the American public. Ellsberg and a colleague, Anthony Russo, secretly photocopied these documents and provided them to members of the US Congress (Circle 2—legislative elites). When Congress, acting at best as conformers, if not as colluders, did nothing with this information, Ellsberg took the personal risk of illegally providing copies of the report to seventeen different responsible media organizations (Circle 2—media elites).

However, Ellsberg himself was greatly influenced by Circle 4 followers—principled activists.

"Without young men going to prison for nonviolent protest against the draft, men that I met on their way to prison, no Pentagon Papers. It wouldn't have occurred to me simply to do something that would put myself in prison for the rest of my life, as I assumed that would do . . . So obviously, that was not an obvious decision to make, except once I'd seen the example of people like Randy Kehler and Bob Eaton and others—and David Harris—who did go to prison to say that this war was wrong, the Vietnam War was wrong, and that they refused to participate in it."

—DANIEL ELLSBERG, in conversation with National Public Radio's (NPR) Dave Davies[2]

De Sales, transforming a noun into a verb, would characterize Ellsberg's decision to copy and distribute the

Pentagon Papers as "Rubiconizing." This draws on the well-known metaphor of Julius Caesar crossing the Rubicon River with his army, an irrevocable act that began the civil war in Rome in 49 BC. To interrupt a prototyrant's progression, at some point, courageous followers will need to cross their own Rubicon.

Ellsberg and Russo were arrested. When Russo was offered a deal if he would turn on Ellsberg, his response, which cited Mahatma Gandhi, was memorable:

"You should not cooperate with evil."

Contagiousness of Courage

What happened next is an example of the social contagiousness of courageous followership that is needed to call out the deceptions and aggression of a prototyrannical regime.

The *New York Times* was initially the only media outlet to begin publishing what became known as the Pentagon Papers. After publishing two installments, the Nixon administration's justice department sued the *Times*, resulting in a federal judge issuing a restraining order to stop further publication. The *Times* complied, which might have killed the story. But the *Washington Post* picked up the baton and published its installment of the Pentagon Papers. The court extended the restraining order to the *Post*, to which they, too, complied.

The free press was now on full alert to perform their constitutional right to responsibly publish segments informing
the public of the real status of the war and the knowing lies
they had been fed by their government. CBS nationwide
aired the story on television, followed by print stories in the
Boston Globe and the *St. Louis Dispatch*, both well-regarded
regional newspapers. Every time a paper was restrained
from printing a further edition, another paper picked up
the baton, including the *Chicago Sun-Times*, the *Los Angeles
Times*, and eleven Knight newspapers.

This was a dazzling display of resistance by the media
segment of the elite circle and an organic emergence of a
coalition of the courageous standing up to the coercive
power of the State. It is truly a moment to be studied and
celebrated for how a free society responded early enough to
the abuse of government power.

Nixon's Prototyrant Behavior

We note—and hear this well—that these acts of resistance were
not taken under a tyrannical regime, which could and would
have summarily shut down these publications and imprisoned
their owners. They were done in the window available before
power was consolidated to the point of absolute control.

This remains the key—to act in the window of opportunity despite real but manageable risks.

These events occurred in 1971. I would argue that they
were ethical preparation for response to the next prototyrannical act of the Nixon administration—the break-in,

burglary, and cover-up of the Democratic National Committee headquarters in the Watergate building in 1972.

Watergate—The Circles of Followers
Unmasking Abuse of Power

The media, specifically the *Washington Post* and its elite publisher, Katherine Graham, again played a key role in exposing the cover-up of the burglary of the Democratic campaign offices by the Committee for the Re-Election of the President (often mocked by the acronym CREEP), and its attempted cover-up by the Nixon White House. But they could not do so alone.

The *Post* reporters Bob Woodward and Carl Bernstein received a stream of tips from a source, who insisted on anonymity, on where to look for evidence of the cover-up. The identity of this source was guessed at but not publicly confirmed for decades. It was the associate director of the FBI, Mark Felt. Despite his elevated status as second-in-command of the FBI, Felt was still a member of the bureaucratic circle of followers (Circle 3), nearly congenitally bound not to cross their political masters—except when supporting their political masters' acts would violate their constitutional duty to uphold the law and protect the nation from enemies within or outside of the State.

Given the severe values conflict, Felt chose to leak the clues that uncovered the damning facts, counting on the journalistic code of ethics not to be outed as the source of those leaks. Courage is not unlimited, so we might count this as a self-protective choice of limited courage that was sufficient to expose corruption.

In the burglary trials that followed, the dominoes began to fall. Those who managed and took part in the break-in (colluder followers) perjured themselves to protect the Office of the President. When one of them, James McCord Jr., confessed to perjury, others began to admit collusion and implicate additional confidantes. As is often the story, those who committed crimes on behalf of the prototyrant began receiving prison sentences, while the prototyrant denied culpability.

During congressional hearings, a White House aide (Circle 1 follower) revealed to the Senate investigating committee that the recording system installed by President Johnson in the Oval Office was still operational and in use. Army Signal Corps technicians (Circle 3) were called in and gave sworn affidavits about the existence of the taping system. The chairman of the Senate Watergate Committee and the special prosecutor (Circle 2) demanded access to the tapes. In an attempt to withhold their release, Nixon, now publicly showing his prototyrannical impulses, ordered the firing of the special prosecutor. In support of the prosecutor, Nixon's attorney general and deputy attorney general (Circles 1 and 2) resigned in protest (courageous followers crossing the Rubicon). The national media joined in clamoring for the release of the tapes.

In the background, while these criminal acts were gradually being revealed, anti–Vietnam War sentiment continued to play out, with massive protests around the country (Circle 5). As Nixon's illegal acts were unmasked, there was no support left for him in the general population, and anti-war activists (Circle 4) used the general loss of trust in the government to further press for the end of the war, which occurred months after Nixon was forced to resign.

In February of 1974, the US House of Representatives (Circle 2—legislative elites) unanimously authorized its judiciary committee to subpoena any information concerning the investigation on whether to impeach Nixon. The Supreme Court (Circle 2—elite judiciary) unanimously ruled that the president had to surrender the tapes. It should be remembered that before the citizenry (Circle 5) had any of this information, it had reelected Nixon to a second term in an electoral college landslide. In the face of this, these public servants were now acting as courageous followers *of the Constitution and the rule of law*. They made a clear choice to no longer continue as conformist or colluder followers to a president and party leader who did not represent the values they were sworn to uphold.

Rather than submit to impeachment by the House of Representatives and the near inevitability of being found guilty by the Senate, Nixon resigned his office and left Washington, DC, on his last flight on the presidential airplane, Air Force One.

Lessons Learned

We cannot, of course, read the preceding events as a morality tale of good always winning over evil. It was a moment in time when the courageous acts of many individuals coalesced into a narrative that stood up to the abuse of political power and won the day. There were no guarantees of this outcome. There never are.

Yet the lessons should be clear: Even in politics, in which loyalty to one's party is nearly sacrosanct, there is still a higher loyalty to the integrity of the nation and its governance. The signs of a political leader emerging who threatens those values and the institutions protecting them can and should be acted on. Once again, this must be done in the window before control over the levers of power is consolidated, closing the avenues of remediation and transformation.

When we follow, at any level of the polity or government, we must bear in mind that above the leaders whom we follow are the values and the institutions designed to keep them serving us. No matter where we are in the circles of followership, we have agency to support those values and institutions. We conform when doing so serves the communal good in which we all have an interest, and we courageously and ethically nonconform if we are being led down a darker path.

It is followers who create their leaders: the good, the bad, and the dangerous. It is courageous followers at every level of the polity, from the streets to the inner sanctum, who tame the worst instincts of power and bring forth its best gifts of public service.

CHAPTER 15

REFLECTIONS ON

POLITICAL FOLLOWING

.

Life is busy. We have much to do to keep things going—our personal finances, our health, our relationships, our journey through this life.

Those of us living in relatively free, democratic countries would greatly prefer to have a selection of competent candidates for the highest offices in our system, give them some support and our vote, and let them get on with the business of governing. We are not on Earth to serve the government. Government is created to serve us, to make it possible to live the life we choose with as much freedom and security as possible.

Yet, we cannot afford to ignore the government and the political processes that form it. If we do, we are more likely to get a government that serves its interests at the expense of ours. If this is true, then we must give some attention to who leads that government and, implicitly, how we choose to follow or not follow them. We are dancing with them, whether in close embrace or from afar.

We all find ourselves in one of the circles around the leader that we and others helped elevate to their current role. If we live in a small community, as I do, we know our school board members, our mayor, our county supervisors, and the elected sheriff or their equivalents in the system in which we live. We may still choose to play in the outer circle and simply be a member of the community, or we may have a reason or cause to play a more intimate and influential role.

In the larger polities of which we are a member—in my instance, the State of Virginia and the United States of America—it is less likely we have close access to those who lead the massive units of government or to the political processes that select them. But at various times and for various reasons, we may have this access. Perhaps we support a cause that has become important in our lives, and we find ourselves in an activist role. Then, to our surprise, the intensity of our activism leads us to an influencer role, perhaps even to become a national spokesperson or a candidate ourselves.

I have a friend whose income is meager and whose energy is limited by age and health. But she is a good observer and writer. Over the years, a major newspaper in her city has accepted opinion pieces she submits for publication. Her views are clear, designed to point to injustice, yet filled with potential solutions rather than mudslinging. The paper now accepts submissions from her several times a month.

Political operatives have been known to read it. When she writes about issues of interest to the governor or a senator of the state, it is likely that staff members will bring it to their attention. She finds herself moving between the roles of citizen and activist. If we use the definition of *elites* as being able to get the attention of those in power, she may even be operating in the outer band of that circle. By extension, should a national political leader display prototyrant behavior, she could potentially gain the attention of her state's elites to call this into question.

The circles of following we have looked at in these pages are descriptive. They do not assign us to an immutable caste. They reflect where we find ourselves in relation to different levels of political leadership, at different points in our lives, and according to the actions we take.

This fluidity applies to political leaders as well. Many begin their journey modestly, or even unintentionally, as it unfolds from their life experiences. A young military veteran feels called to have their country provide better veteran care. A displaced factory worker feels the need to make heartland voices represented in Congress. They throw their hat into the ring and, through skill, passion, sponsorship, and timing, find themselves in the government they sought to influence.

These emerging political leaders bring with them the proclivities of their upbringing, personality, culture, traumas, passions, worldviews, and varying capacities for self-reflection and growth. They themselves may have begun as a citizen in the outer circle of how their society organizes itself, or they may have been the scion of a political dynasty. This shapes their leadership instincts. Some of those experiences will make them a natural leader for a specific context at a specific moment in history. If they are successful, they will be re-elected and serve within the existing institutions of government.

As political leaders, they have entered a dynamic field that they will attempt to influence and change, while at the same time, it influences and changes them. We benefit if they have a moral and psychological center that resists being changed in ways that bring out the darker side of power, but most cannot do this alone. It is the character and the courage of their followers that help steady them as the field dynamics buffet them around with pressures and temptations. One member with whom I worked, told his senior staff, with both sagacity and trepidation, their primary responsibility was not to let him do anything that would result in a prison sentence.

If the political leader has latent narcissistic and autocratic tendencies, these will grow if the ground—the context—is fertile. It remains with their followers to manage these tendencies so their leaders stay within the bounds of serving their governance role. When these tendencies threaten to break through those bounds, it is time for followers to act.

The combined chart that follows gives us a comparative thumbnail sketch of the world as it is experienced across the five circles of followers. But remember, this is only a memory jogger; it is not a substitute for the deeper understanding and work needed to keep political leaders serving us rather than devouring us, as tyrants throughout history have done.

CHARACTERISTICS OF EACH CIRCLE OF FOLLOWERS

	Populace	Activists	Bureaucrats	Elites	Confidants
Available Information	Autocrat pronouncements, popular media	Movement messaging and specialized media	Political appointee briefings, data agency collects	Confidential briefings, market maker insights	Autocrat's musings, rantings, strategies, and instructions
Incentives to Follow	Enhanced social identity and material promises	Purposeful life, enacting a vision	Organization inertia, job retention, chance to make an impact	Hope for influence, retaining access and privileges	Loyalty, perks, and rewards of power, consequences of loss of power
Vulnerability	Susceptible to charisma/wish for a savior	The blindness of a true believer	Lost sense of moral accountability	Belief they can control the prototyrant	Loyalty to the person, not the office
Risks	Social and economic costs of dissent	Persecution by the establishment, disapproval from the movement	Demotion, sidelining, and termination	Loss of own power base or access to and support of autocrat	Complicity in illegal acts, becoming a scapegoat or a danger to the autocrat
Communication Channels	Mass rallies and social media	Social media followings	Formal channels and expert opinions	Private communiqués and audiences, access to top-tier media	Private conversations, personal contact info, inner circle briefings, and eyes-only communications
Courage Needed	Standing apart from the crowd	Recognizing when backing the wrong leader	Candor within and outside of channels	Taking displeasing positions	Working with others to curtail tyrannical inclinations
Power to Influence	Collective—mass shows of support or disaffection	Ability to shape messages/support positive leaders	Formal assessments, briefings, and anonymous leaks	Deep pocket financing, control of institutions that can support or oppose	Last person in the room, final touches on communications and policies

Look around. Pay attention. Where are you in relation to political leaders? Where are they in the continuum from leader to tyrant? Do what is yours to do. Together, courageous followers may break the cycle of the rise of political tyrants. One distant day, perhaps we can make them a relic of the long, difficult history of toxic political leadership and the human misery it creates. For now, we can at least apply "the brakes" on toxicity while supporting healthier forms of leadership. Start where you are, do what you can, and work with others who are courageous allies.

Act while the window is open, and the fresh breezes of political freedom still find their way into the halls of government.

ACKNOWLEDGMENTS

Writing a book is a paradox. It is a solitary activity that is firmly embedded in community. While working on this project these past several years, I have become indebted to many people who helped make the book better than I could have done on my own. While not quite as long as the rolling credits in a Hollywood film, neither is the list short.

I will start by thanking the editor and publisher of my two prior books on followership, Steve Piersanti of Berrett-Koehler. While BK wasn't well positioned to publish this third leg of the trilogy, Steve spent considerable time helping me sharpen the focus of the book and shaping it into a more reader-friendly experience.

Due to the wonders of handheld technology, I often dictated new observations into my phone for later transcription.

While these may have caught my insights in real time, at some point, they needed to be woven into a structure that painted a clear picture for the reader. Mary Carnahan, a talented book designer, is also a good friend and editor. We spent many hours working out the sequence and aggregation of these into discrete chapters with decent segues. Mary rendered the graphics that help a reader visualize the relationship between a political leader and their followers, as well as track the progression of autocratic leadership. She and another designer friend, Debbie Witt, lent their sharp eyes to the creation of the cover of the book.

During the pandemic of 2021–2023, when work and revenue dried up for me, along with millions of others, my friend Carl Barney provided funds that allowed me to continue working on the project. The book's support for non-tyrannical government overlaps with his own philosophy of freedom from government coercion.

Foundational to this work is the global followership community that has grown up over the last few years. I won't call out the names of many good friends and colleagues in this community, but I deeply appreciate their commitment to understanding and elevating effective and ethical followership.

One of the activists in this community is also a close supporter of my followership work in general and this project in particular. Sharna Fabiano has had my back in seeing this project through to completion and beyond. Her own work in followership is gorgeous and committed. I am grateful for her allyship every step of the way.

Another torch bearer in the followership community is Alain de Sales. He stood up and facilitated the teachingfollowerscourage.com community for several years. Alain drew on my work for his dissertation, and I now draw on his. Lead and follow.

Behind the scenes, critical work gets done with little glory. Two of these "engine room" stalwarts are my long-term colleagues, Dario Orlando Fernandez and Jenny Dao. Dario has too many talents to list, from research to graphics to platform security and translation. Jenny has provided business continuity and personal peace of mind over all matters administrative and financial. Both are cherished for their friendship, dedication and effectiveness.

Another long-term publishing supporter is Johanna Vondeling. With patience and thoroughness, Johanna guided me through the world of contemporary publishing options and stayed with me while the process hit shoals that needed a steady hand to navigate.

An invaluable service was performed by deeply experienced readers of the manuscript at its various stages. One long-term truth-telling supporter and one new, Steven Bosacker and Tim Carrington, read a mid-process version and gave me candid feedback that I needed to ground my observations in more and better examples. Thank you for saving me from embarrassment. Two women with extensive experience in the federal bureaucracy, Cindy Smith and Bea Edwards, helped me fill in the text with their lived examples of courage in navigating the politics and perils of these massive hierarchies and their entrenched cultures.

A most sensible ally from the Federal Executive Institute, Michael Belcher, contributed to both substantive and stylistic improvements.

Another champion was Betty Rivard, a long-lost friend who re-emerged in the nick of time to read the still-developing text from the perspective of the political science background we shared in the long-ago sixties. Going back even further, David Greene, my childhood friend and political activist par excellence, was supportive of my aims while questioning the worldview I hold that differs from his.

Alan Briskin, the man who is too young to be my mentor but nevertheless performs a reasonable impersonation of this, watched the development of this book in our monthly conversations. He has an uncanny way of helping me better understand what it is I am doing.

Friends and family who learned of my topic would send me germane clips of articles and podcasts they came across. These include my old pal Jay (Ira) Hurwitz (note, I'm Ira Jay) and my newfound "mishpachah" Michael Blocker and Merrie Blocker Merlo. My connection to them is Elizabeth Blocker Ebaugh, the love that came into my life while writing this book, deeply understanding its place in who I am and why I do what I do.

The final editorial tribute goes to Rick Shapiro, my successor at the nonpartisan Congressional Management Foundation. Rick and I served in the same nonpartisan capacity. He viscerally understands the validity of working to improve "both sides of the aisle." His unerring eye and ear helped put important finishing touches on the book.

Lastly, books only get into the world with help, and even dedication, from their publishers. I am grateful to Maggie Langrick for recognizing the need for this book and bringing it into the world under the Wonderwell imprint. It is now in the good hands of Tanya Hall and the Greenleaf Book Group, which is Wonderwell's new home. Their staff run a polished operation in bringing a book to life and getting it into your hands.

My gratitude to all. If I have omitted anyone in error, please accept my apology.

IRA CHALEFF | June 2024

WORKS CITED

INTRODUCTION

1. Alain de Sales, "Breaking Toxic Triangles: How Courageous Followers Stand up to Destructive Leadership" (doctoral thesis, Swinburne University of Technology, 2020), https://researchbank.swinburne.edu.au/file/32cf6407-c0b0-4d24-a953-0db1a73db3d7/1/Alain_deSales_Thesis.pdf.

2. One example of this is an article by Samantha Power, "How Democracy Can Win," *Foreign Affairs*, March/April 2023.

3. Imam Imam, "Obasanjo's Aides Worked Against 3rd Term," AllAfrica.com, October 25, 2008, https://allafrica.com/stories/200810270486.html.

CHAPTER 1

1. Barbara Kellerman, *Followership: How Followers Are Creating Change and Changing Leaders* (Brighton, MA: Harvard Business Review Press, 2008).

CHAPTER 2

1. Farah Stockman, "He Made His Country Rich, but Something Has Gone Wrong with the System," *The New York Times*, April 12, 2023, https://www.nytimes.com/2023/04/12/opinion/international-world/singapore-autocracy-democracy.html.

2. Serhii Plokhy, *Yalta: The Price of Peace* (New York: Viking, 2010).

3. Maayan Lubell, "Protests Grip Israel Ahead of Historic Supreme Court Session," Reuters, September 11, 2023, https://www.reuters.com/world/middle-east/israel-edge-ahead-supreme-court-session-judicial-overhaul-2023-09-11/.

4. Maximilian Weber, *The Theory of Social and Economic Organization* (New York: Oxford University Press, 1948).

5. "Turkey Could Be on the Brink of Dictatorship," *The Economist*, January 19, 2023, https://www.economist.com/leaders/2023/01/19/turkey-could-be-on-the-brink-of-dictatorship?ppccampaignID=&ppcadID=&ppcgclID=&utm_medium=cpc.adword.pd&utm_source=google&ppccampaignID=17210591673&ppcadID=&utm_campaign=a.22brand_pmax&utm_content=conversion.direct-response.anonymous&gad_source=1&gclid=Cj0KCQjwncWvBhD_ARIsAEb2HW_YUL3nsmJZjpCukUWgvxaDIcjFkA4GZQhdryXMLYfHIHdmRN9-jt8aAhpKEALw_wcB&gclsrc=aw.ds.

6. Roger Cohen, "The Making of Vladimir Putin," *The New York Times*, March 22, 2022, https://www.nytimes.com/2022/03/26/world/europe/vladimir-putin-russia.html.

7. Roger Cohen, "The Making of Vladimir Putin," *The New York Times*, March 22, 2022, https://www.nytimes.com/2022/03/26/world/europe/vladimir-putin-russia.html.

8. Roger Cohen, "The Making of Vladimir Putin," *The New York Times*, March 22, 2022, https://www.nytimes.com/2022/03/26/world/europe/vladimir-putin-russia.html.

9. Julian Jackson, "Charles de Gaulle Reconsidered," August 28, 2018, in *History Extra*, podcast, https://podcasts.apple.com/fi/podcast/charles-de-gaulle-reconsidered/id256580326?i=1000418665036.

CHAPTER 3

1. Max Weber, "Politics as a Vocation," essay, January 28, 1919.

CHAPTER 4

1. A.H. Maslow, *Maslow on Management* (Hoboken, NJ: John Wiley & Sons, 1998) 266–267.

2. "The 'World's Coolest Dictator' Wins a Second Term," *The Economist*, February 10, 2024.

3. Sari Horwitz, "Unlikely Allies," *The Washington Post*, August 15, 2015.

4. Johnny Dodd, "David Duke's Godson Derek Black Fully Embraced White Nationalism — Until Friends Opened His Eyes," *People Magazine*, September 13, 2018, https://people.com/books/david-dukes-godson-derek-black-fully-embraced-white-nationalism-until-friends-opened-his-eyes/.

5. Robert Schatz, Ervin Staub, and Howard Lavine, "On the Varieties of National Attachment: Blind Versus Constructive Patriotism," *Political Psychology* 20, no. 1 (Mar 1999).

6. Robert Schatz, Ervin Staub, and Howard Lavine, "On the Varieties of National Attachment: Blind Versus Constructive Patriotism," *Political Psychology* 20, no. 1 (Mar 1999).

CHAPTER 5

1. Elias Canetti, *Crowds and Power* (Berlin: Claassen Verlag, 1960).

2. "How Young Sudanese Are Still Fighting for Democracy," *The Economist*, January 19, 2023, https://www.economist.com/middle-east-and-africa/2023/01/19/how-young-sudanese-are-still-fighting-for-democracy.

CHAPTER 6

1. Assaf Sharon, "This Obstinate Little Man," *The New York Review of Books*, November 4, 2021.

2. Alma Guillermoprieto, "Nicaragua's Dreadful Duumvirate," *The New York Review of Books,* December 16, 2021.

3. Saul Alinsky, *Rules for Radicals* (New York: Random House, 1971).

4. *The Week* staff, "The 'Agent Provocateur' Who Infiltrated Occupy Wall Street," *The Week*, January 8, 2015.

5. Juan Francisco Fuentes, "Shirt Movements in Interwar Europe: A Totalitarian Fashion," *Ler Historia* 72 (2018): 151.

CHAPTER 7

1. Michael Leo Owens, Tom Clark, and Adam Glynn, "Where Do Police Departments Get Their Military-Style Gear? Here's What We Don't Know," *The Washington Post*, July 20, 2022. https://www.washingtonpost.com/politics/2020/07/20/where-do-police-departments-get-their-military-style-gear-heres-what-we-dont-know/

CHAPTER 9

1. Gordon MacKenzie, *Orbiting the Giant Hairball* (New York: Viking, 1998): 33.

2. The Centre for Army Leadership, "A British Army Followership Doctrine Note," 2023, https://www.army.mod.uk/media/23250/20230810-followership_doctrine_note-final_-v11.pdf.

3. Ira Chaleff, *Intelligent Disobedience* (New York: MJF Books, 2015): 92.

4. "Constructive Dissent Awards," American Foreign Service Association, https://afsa.org/constructive-dissent-awards.

CHAPTER 10

1. Lyndon B. Johnson, letter to Dr. Martin Luther King Jr., Collection LBJ-WHCF: White House Central Files (Johnson Administration), March 18, 1965, https://www.docsteach.org/documents/document/lbj-to-mlk.

2. Nelson Mandela, *Long Walk to Freedom* (Boston: Little, Brown and Company, 2013).

3. Barbara Kellerman, *Followership: How Followers Are Creating Change and Changing Leaders* (Brighton, MA: Harvard Business Review Press, 2008).

4. Tom Parfitt, "Mikhail Khodorkovsky Sentenced to 14 Years in Prison," *The Guardian*, December 30, 2010, https://www.theguardian.com/world/2010/dec/30/mikhail-khodorkovsky-jail-term.

CHAPTER 11

1. Tom Burns, "Spaniards March to Back Democracy," *The Washington Post*, February 28, 1981, https://www.washingtonpost.com/archive/politics/1981/02/28/spaniards-march-to-back-democracy/fd13c7b2-5e74-48a8-81be-56fb6e460de1/.

2. David Edmonds and Nigel Warburton, "Seth Lazar on Philosophy in the Age of AI," September 27, 2023, in *Philosophy Bites*, podcast.

3. Kat Stoeffel, "13 Pop Stars Who Sang for Dictators," *New York Magazine*, July 3, 2013, https://www.thecut.com/2013/07/13-pop-stars-who-sang-for-dictators.html.

4. Burns, "Spaniards March."

CHAPTER 12

1. "Nicaraguan Revolutionary Hero Dies in Jail as Ortega Political Prisoner," *The Tico Times*, February 13, 2022, https://ticotimes.net/2022/02/13/nicaraguan-revolutionary-hero-dies-in-jail-as-ortega-political-prisoner.

CHAPTER 13

1. "Seneca," *Encyclopedia Britannica*, https://www.britannica.com/biography/Lucius-Annaeus-Seneca-Roman-philosopher-and-statesman.

2. Hugh O'Connell, "What Was Watergate? Here Are 14 Facts That Explain Everything," *The Journal*, June 24, 2012, https://www.thejournal.ie/what-was-watergate-14-facts-richard-nixon-494970-Jun2012/.

3. Scott Allen, "Dr. John Dugan—Praxis," September 21, 2020, in *Phronesis*, podcast.

4. Emma Burrows, "Kremlin Foe Alexei Navalny's Team Confirms His death and Says His Mother Is Searching for His Body," AP News, February 17, 2024, https://apnews.com/article/russia-alexei-navalny-death-opposition-leader-37da0915157576372d6493be7ad04b5c.

5. Jerrold Post, "Explaining Saddam," statement before the House Armed Services Committee, December 1990, PBS *Frontline*, https://www.pbs.org/wgbh/pages/frontline/shows/unscom/readings/post.html.

6. Jaroslaw Anders, "Hansel and Gretel in Belarus," *The New York Review of Books*, June 10, 2021.

7. Andrew Bibby, "1940, Franklin D. Roosevelt's Unprecedented Run for a Third Term," Constituting America, https://constitutingamerica.org/1940-franklin-d-roosevelts-unprecedented-run-for-a-third-term-guest-essayist-andrew-bibby/.

8. Bibby, "1940."

CHAPTER 14

1. De Sales, "Breaking Toxic Triangles."

2. Dave Davies, "How the Pentagon Papers Changed Public Perception of the War in Vietnam," NPR, June 18, 2021.